United States
Department of
Agriculture

Forest
Service

North Central
Research Station

Resource Bulletin
NC-265

Pulpwood Production in the North-Central Region, 2004

Ronald J. Piva

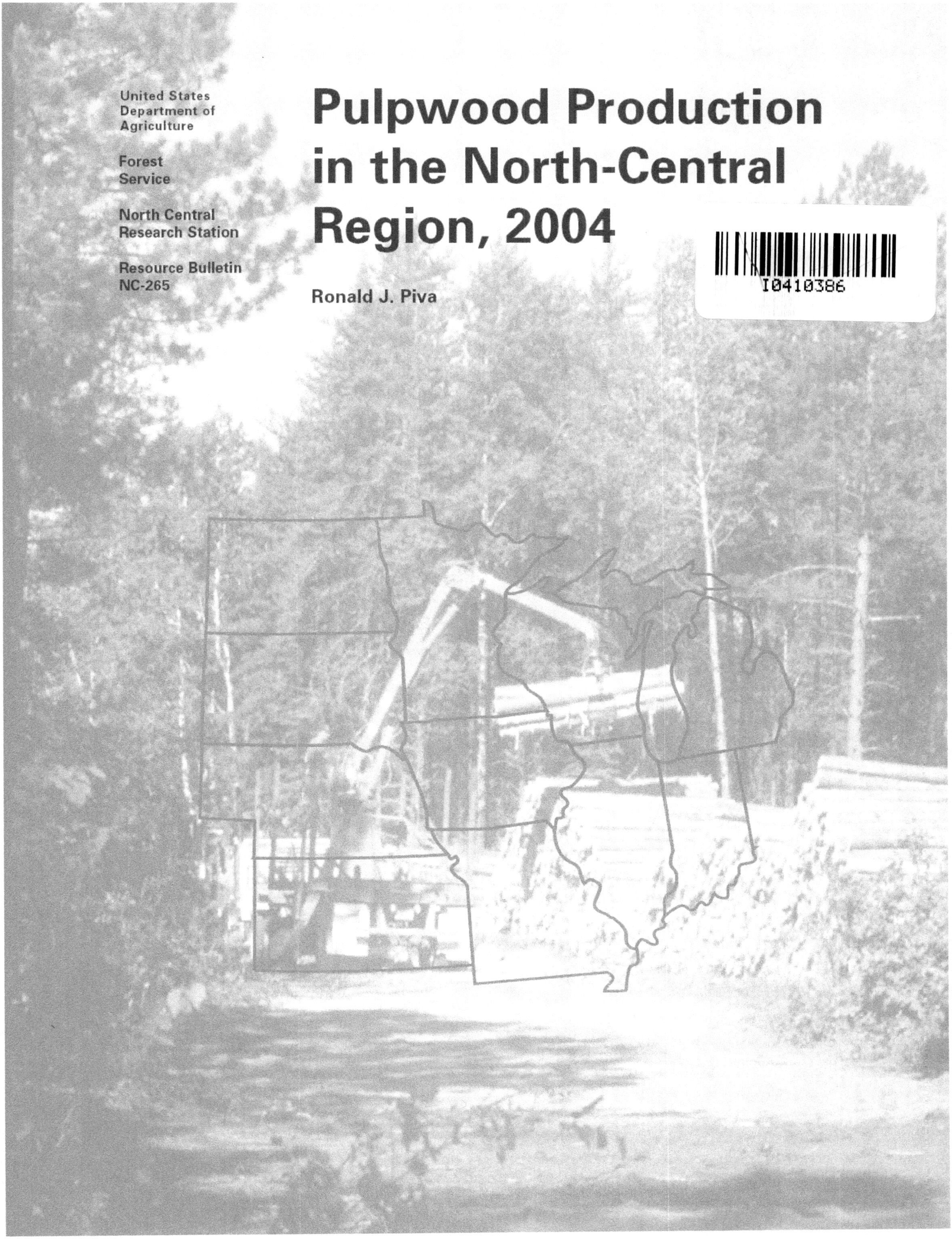

North Central Research Station
Forest Service—U.S. Department of Agriculture
1992 Folwell Avenue
St. Paul, Minnesota 55108
2006
www.ncrs.fs.fed.us

Table of Contents

Pulpwood Production in the North-Central Region, 2004

Ronald J. Piva

NOTE: This report includes all primary products made from reconstituted wood fiber. In addition to wood pulp, this includes particleboard and engineered lumber products made from chips, shavings, wafers, flakes, strands, and sawdust. This report presents the production of the raw fiber material delivered to mills. Thus, these data report only that portion of the timber harvest used as raw material and do not necessarily reflect the volume of growing stock harvested.

Ronald J. Piva, Forester, received a B.S. in forest management from the University of Missouri-Columbia. He joined the Forest Service in 1987 and has been working with the North Central Station's Forest Inventory and Analysis unit since.

Pulpwood constitutes more than half the industrial timber products harvested annually in the Lake States (Michigan, Minnesota, and Wisconsin) and is an important product in the Central States (Illinois, Indiana, Iowa, and Missouri) and the Plains States (Kansas, Nebraska, North Dakota, and South Dakota).

Current detailed information about pulpwood production[1] is necessary for intelligent planning and decisionmaking in wood procurement, forest resource management, forest industry development, and scientific studies.

Since 1979, logs, bolts, and wood residue used in manufacturing flakeboard, waferboard, oriented strandboard, and medium density fiberboard have been included in this annual report. Engineered lumber was first included in this report in 1992. Together, these products are called particleboard, and all mills manufacturing these boards are called particleboard mills in this report. Wood used at particleboard mills is identical or nearly identical to wood used at pulp mills; therefore, including this wood in our study provides a more accurate estimate of demand for pulpwood-like material.

Particleboard mills were in their infancy before 1979 and used primarily aspen and wood residue. Therefore, data for these mills do not distort roundwood use trends for other species or preclude comparing 2004 survey results with those of 1978 and previous years.

Pulp and particleboard mills using timber from the North Central States in 2004 reported their pulpwood receipts[2] by species group and county of origin. This report presents the results of the survey, analyzes the data, compares results with those of 2003 and earlier years, and discusses trends in pulpwood production and use.

The Lake States, Central States, and Plains States are discussed separately because the timber types in each area are different, the flow of wood between the areas is nominal, and more detailed data on pulpwood production and receipts in the Central and Plains States might reveal the operations of individual mills. This is the 46th

---

[1] *Pulpwood production, determined from mill receipts, is the annual volume of pulpwood cut, plus the annual wood residue volume produced by sawmills, veneer mills, etc. used for pulp, particleboard, waferboard, oriented strandboard, medium density fiberboard, or engineered lumber.*

[2] *Pulpwood receipts are the volumes of wood received by mills in a specific State or region, regardless of the geographic source.*

annual report of the pulpwood harvest in Lake States counties, the 45th annual report of the Central States harvest, and the 12th report of the pulpwood harvest in the Plains States.

Several mills purchase their pulpwood based on weight rather than volume. Factors used to convert green tons of pulpwood to standard cord equivalents are shown in the appendix.

When new surveys are completed, errors and omissions from previous surveys are corrected. As a result of our ongoing efforts to improve the survey's efficiency and reliability, changes may have been made to the previous survey's data. All comparisons and analysis in this report are based on the reprocessed data from earlier surveys, which may not match earlier published data.

LAKE STATES

PRODUCTION

- Pulpwood production in the Lake States rose from 9.5 million cords[3] in 2003 to 9.8 million cords in 2004, an increase of more than 3 percent. Overall, 90 percent came from roundwood (including chips from roundwood) and 10 percent came from the residue[4] of wood-using plants.

- Aspen remained the dominant species harvested for pulpwood in the Lake States in 2004 with 3.6 million cords or 41 percent of the total roundwood. Other important species harvested for pulpwood in 2004 were soft maple (937 thousand cords), hard maple (883 thousand cords), white birch (629 thousand cords), jack pine (517 thousand cords), and balsam fir (324 thousand cords) (table 1 and fig. 1).

- Softwood roundwood production remained at 1.7 million cords. Pulpwood production from softwood residues increased by more than 12 percent to 511 thousand cords in 2004.

- Hardwood roundwood production increased by almost 5 percent, for 6.8 million cords in 2003 to 7.1 million cords in 2004. From 2003 to 2004, pulpwood production from hardwood residues decreased by almost 12 percent.

- Whole-tree chip[5] (WTC) production, at 799 thousand cords, made up 8 percent of the total pulpwood production in the Lake States in 2004—an increase of more than 40 percent from 2003 (fig. 2).

- Aspen was the predominant species used in WTC in 2004 with 252 thousand cords or 32

---

[3] All references to cords are in standard cords. A standard cord is 128 cubic feet of wood, bark, and air space.

[4] Residue is the byproduct from sawmills, veneer mills, cooperage mills, and other wood-using mills that is used for pulping and particleboard. Residues include slabs, edgings, veneer cores, sawdust, fines, woodflour, and chips manufactured from slabs, edgings, and veneer cores.

[5] Pulpwood produced from chipping entire trees (all portions of the trees above ground, except the stumps).

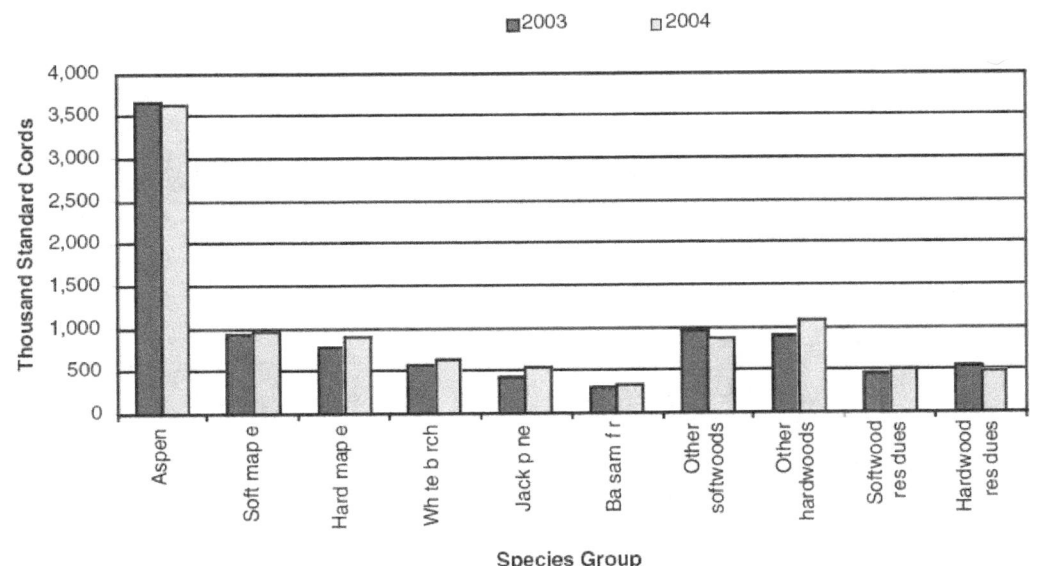

■ 2003 □ 2004

Figure 1.—*Lake States pulpwood production by species group and residues, 2003-2004.*

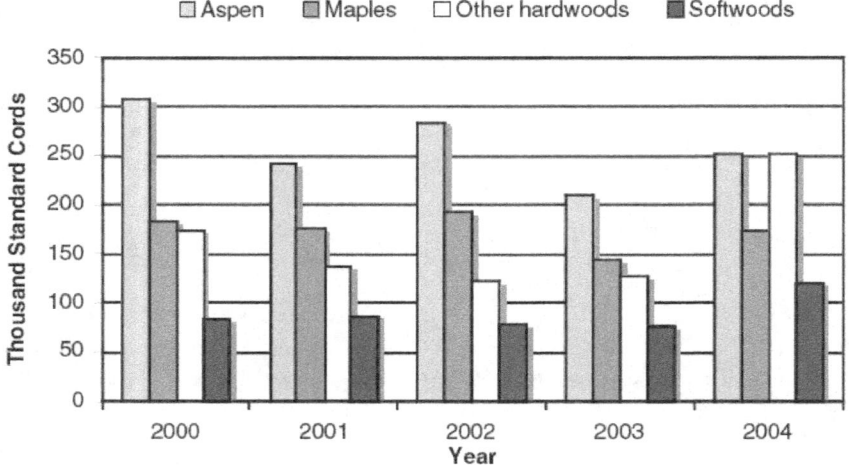

percent of the total WTC production. Jack pine, at 109 thousand cords, was the predominant softwood species used in WTC in 2004 and accounted for 14 percent of the total WTC production.

• Michigan was the major producer of WTC in the Lake States in 2004 with 487 thousand cords (61 percent of the WTC production) (fig. 3).

Michigan

• The total output of wood material for pulpwood production in Michigan increased by 4 percent, from 3.0 million cords in 2003 to 3.1 million cords in 2004. Pulpwood production from roundwood increased by 6 percent while production from residues decreased by almost 9 percent (fig. 4 and tables 2 and 3).

• The Western Upper Peninsula remained the top pulpwood-producing region in the State in 2004 with 39 percent of the total roundwood harvested (fig. 5 and tables 4 and 5).

Minnesota

• Pulpwood production increased by 76 thousand cords, almost 3 percent, between 2003 and 2004. Roundwood pulpwood production increased by almost 2 percent, and pulpwood produced from mill residues increased by more than 23 percent (fig. 6).

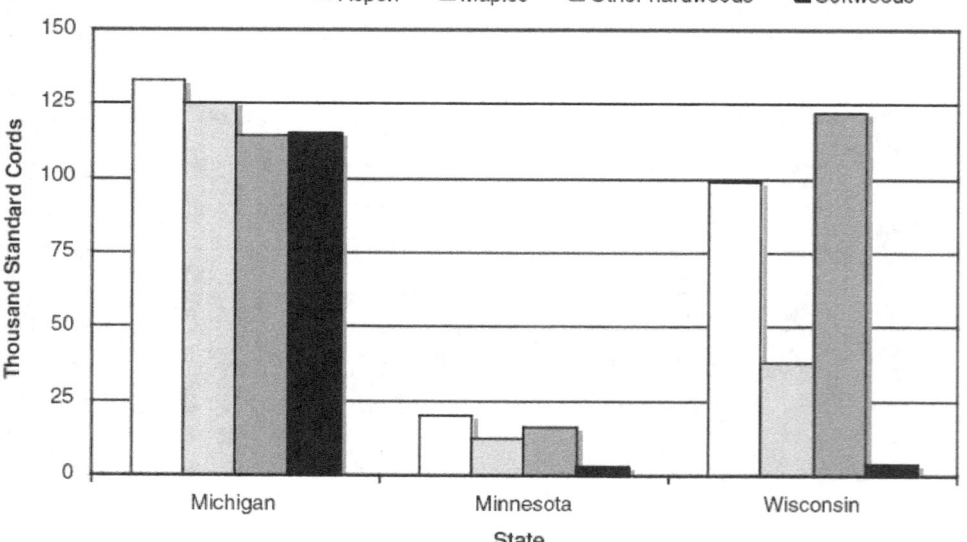

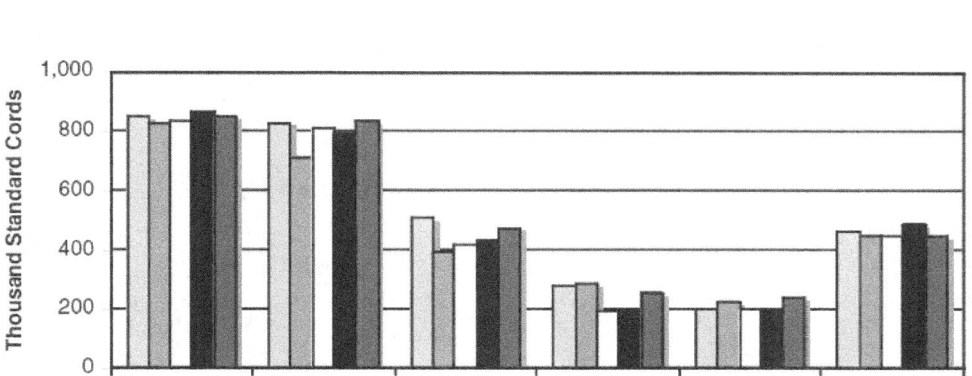

Figure 4.—*Michigan pulpwood production by species group and residues, 2000-20004.*

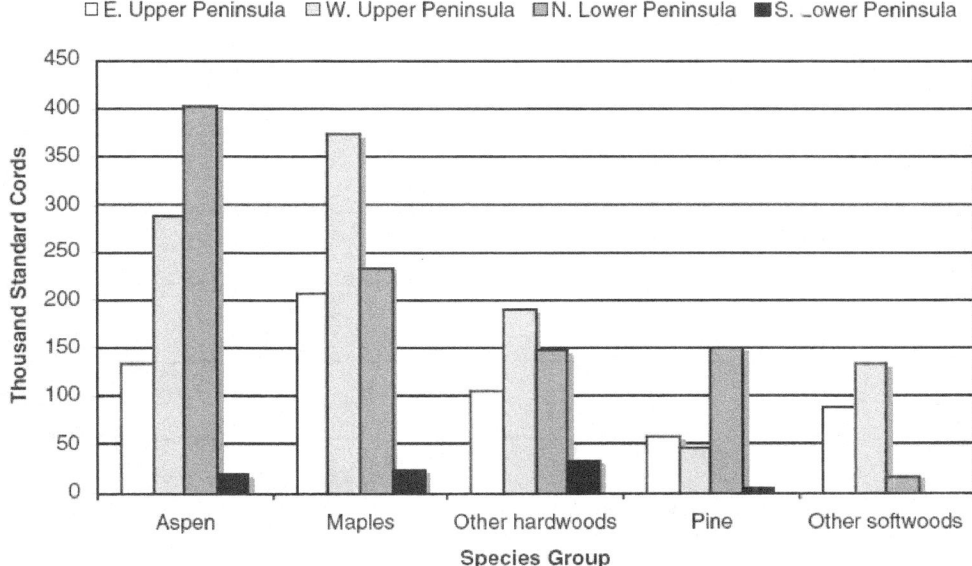

Figure 5.—*Michigan roundwood pulpwood production by Forest Survey Unit and species groups, 2004.*

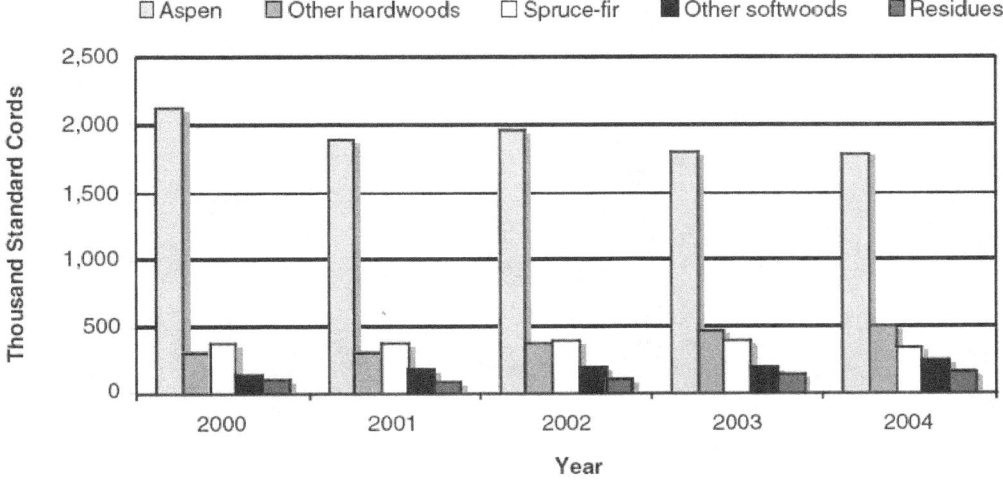

Figure 6.—*Minnesota pulpwood production by species group and residues, 2000-2004.*

- Aspen accounted for 62 percent of all the roundwood harvested for pulpwood in Minnesota in 2004.

- The Aspen-Birch and the Northern Pine Forest Survey Units were the top pulpwood-producing roundwood regions in the State in 2004, each supplying 1.3 million cords of roundwood for pulp (fig. 7 and table 6).

Wisconsin

- Pulpwood production in Wisconsin increased by 4 percent, from 3.5 million cords in 2003 to 3.7 million cords in 2004. Pulpwood production from roundwood increased by 4 percent, and production from residues increased by 2 percent (fig. 8).

- The Northwestern and Northeastern Forest Survey Units remained the top producers of roundwood for pulping in the State with 1.3 million cords and 1.2 million cords, respectively (fig. 9 and table 7).

Harvesting Intensity

- In the following figures, the distribution of the harvest is shown in two ways: first, the amount of pulpwood cut relative to the growing-stock volume in each of five major pulpwood species (fig. 10); second, the amount of pulpwood relative to commercial timberland area (fig. 11).

Figure 7.—*Minnesota roundwood pulpwood production by Forest Survey Unit and species group, 2004.*

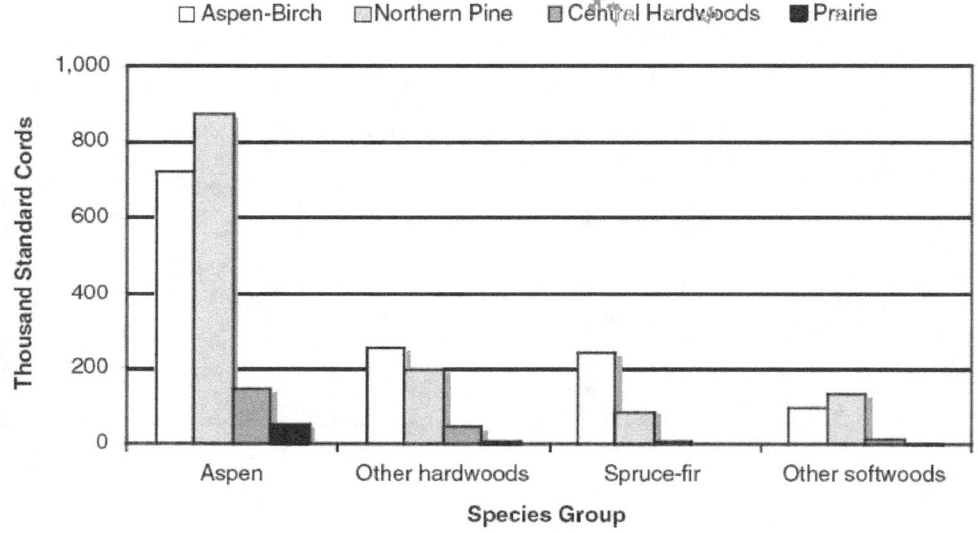

Figure 8.—*Wisconsin pulpwood production by species group and residues, 2000-2004.*

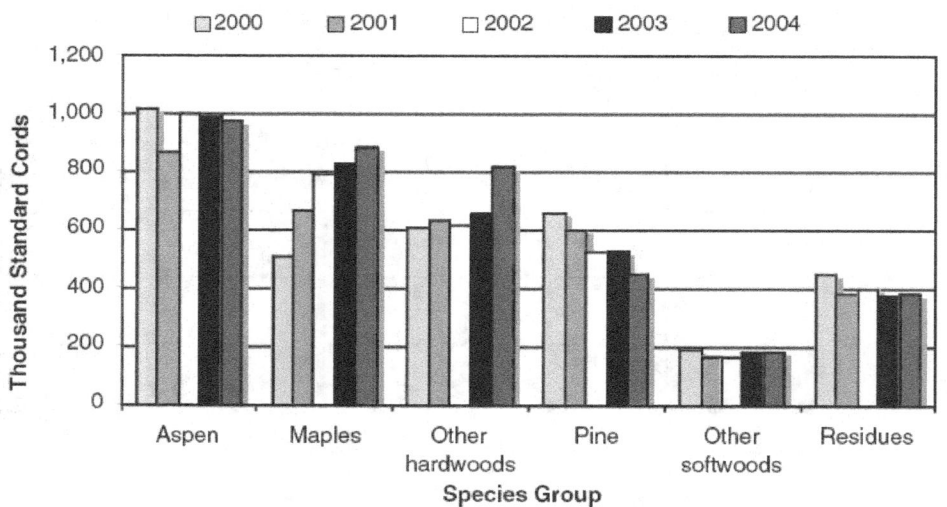

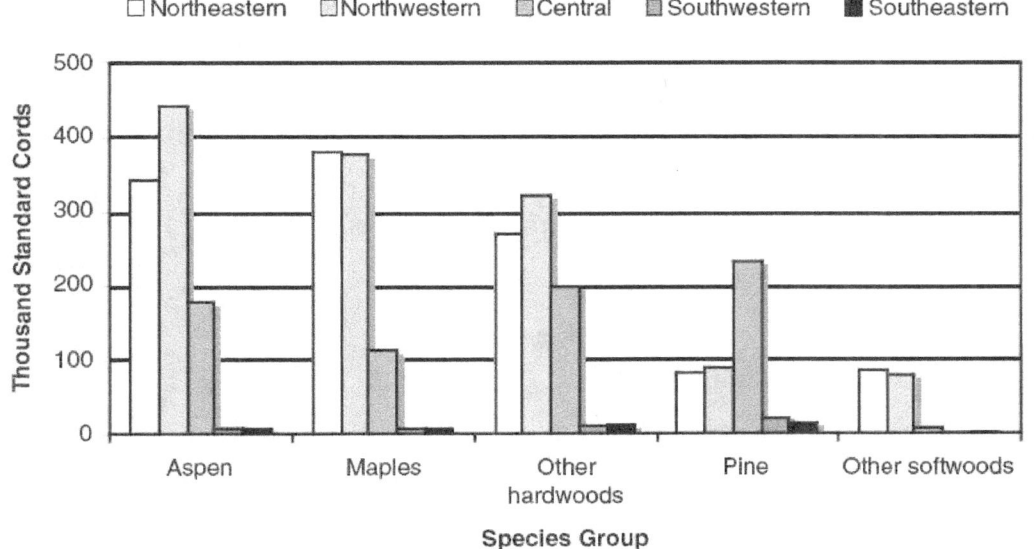

Figure 9.—*Wisconsin roundwood pulpwood production by Forest Survey Unit and species group, 2004.*

Aspen

Figure 10.—*Cords of roundwood pulpwood (including chips from roundwood) harvested per 1,000 cords of growing-stock volume for each of five principal pulpwood species by Forest Survey Unit, 2004.*

White Birch

Jack Pine

8

Soft Maple

Hard Maple

Lake States

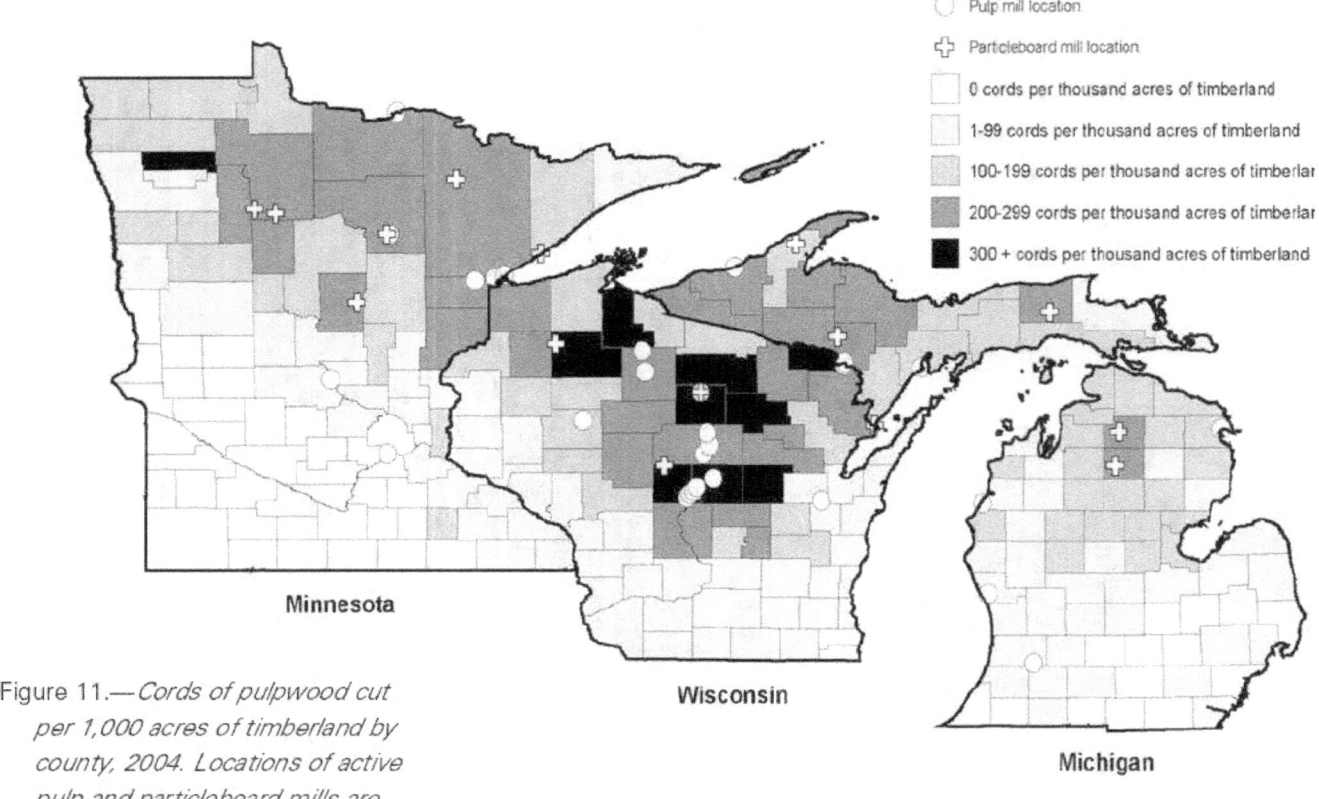

Pulp mill location
Particleboard mill location
0 cords per thousand acres of timberland
1-99 cords per thousand acres of timberland
100-199 cords per thousand acres of timberland
200-299 cords per thousand acres of timberland
300 + cords per thousand acres of timberland

Minnesota

Wisconsin

Michigan

Figure 11.—*Cords of pulpwood cut per 1,000 acres of timberland by county, 2004. Locations of active pulp and particleboard mills are shown.*

RECEIPTS

- In 2004, 29 wood pulp and 15 particleboard mills in the Lake States acquired 10.2 million cords of pulpwood, an increase of 3 percent from the year before. Aspen roundwood was processed at 35 of the 44 pulp and particleboard plants in 2004 (table 8).

- In 2004, Michigan supplied wood to 35 mills, Wisconsin supplied 34 mills, and Minnesota supplied 24 mills.

- Imports of roundwood to Lake States pulp and particleboard mills increased by 5 percent, while mill residue imports decreased by 15 percent between 2003 and 2004. Total imports of all wood material in 2004 were 484 thousand cords, an increase of 3 percent from 2003. Canada contributed 94 percent of the total imports.

Michigan

- The seven Michigan pulp mills, three OSB mills, one particleboard mill, and one molded strandwood mill consumed almost 3.1 million cords in 2004, just 12 thousand cords more than in the previous year. Twelve percent of the total wood material consumed was imported from out of State. Wisconsin supplied 70 percent of the imported wood material.

Minnesota

- The eight pulp mills, five OSB mills, and one laminated structural lumber mill in Minnesota consumed 3.5 million cords in 2004, an increase of almost 4 percent from 2003. Pulp and particleboard mills in Minnesota acquired 19 percent of their raw material from out-of-State sources. Wisconsin supplied almost half of the imported wood material.

Wisconsin

- The 14 pulp mills, 2 OSB mills, and 2 particle-board mills in Wisconsin consumed 3.6 million cords in 2004, an increase of 5 percent from 2003. Almost 15 percent of the total receipts were imported. Of the total wood material imported, 55 percent was brought in from Michigan.

INDUSTRY TRENDS AND ANALYSIS

Pulp Mills

For this section, pulp mill products include wood fiber products such as paper, paperboard, hardboard, insulation board, and medium-density fiberboard. All of these products are manufactured from wood that has been reduced to individual fibers, small fiber bundles, or fiber parts that are subsequently formed into a mat. Wood material from the Lake States sent to mills in other States and Canada is included.

- Of the 9.8 million cords of pulpwood produced in the Lake States in 2004, 7.1 million cords (72 percent) were used for wood pulp products. Overall, 88 percent came from roundwood and 12 percent came from mill residues.

- Principal species harvested for pulp in the Lake States in 2004 were aspen (1.8 million

cords), hard maple (843 thousand cords), soft maple (834 thousand cords), and white birch (501 thousand cords) (fig. 12).

- Hardwoods were still the mainstay of the pulp mills in the region in 2004: hardwood round-wood contributed more than 68 percent of total raw material, and hardwood residues supplied another 6 percent.

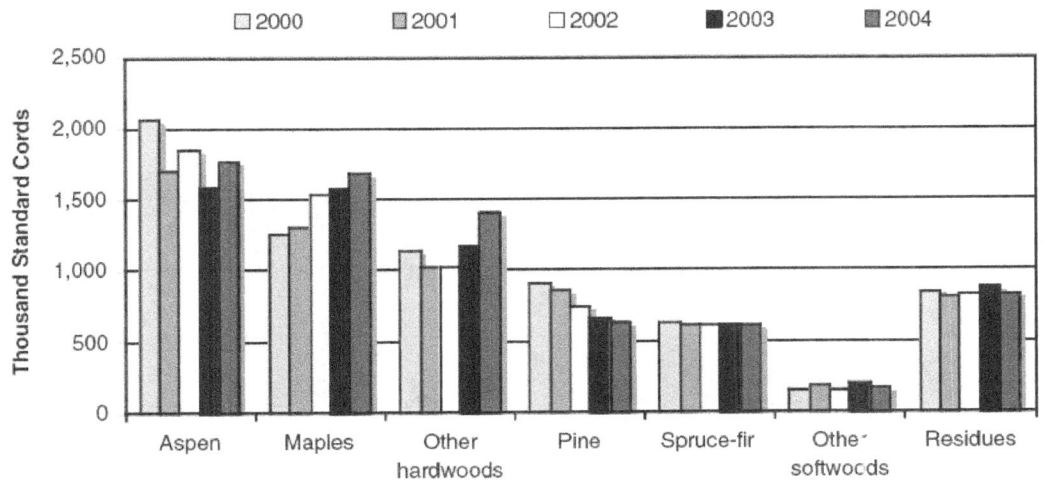

Figure 12.—
Pulpwood production in the Lake States for pulp by species group and residues, 2000-2004

Table A.—*Lake States pulpwood production for pulp mills during 2000-2004*

Product form and species group	Production				
	2000	2001	2002	2003	2004
	--------(Thousand cords)--------				
Roundwood					
Softwoods	1,674	1,658	1,500	1,480	1,391
Aspen	2,057	1,707	1,854	1,588	1,768
Other hardwoods	2,385	2,320	2,573	2,744	3,086
Residues	852	804	825	880	832
Total	6,968	6,488	6,753	6,693	7,077

- Hardwood roundwood harvested from the Lake States for pulp mills increased by 12 percent between 2003 and 2004, while Lake States softwood roundwood production decreased by 6 percent. Softwood residues generated by Lake States primary wood-processing facilities, and used by pulp mills, increased by 5 percent, and hardwood residues decreased by almost 15 percent during the same period.

- Average daily wood pulp production in 2004 remained at the 2003 level of 14.7 thousand tons of pulp per day (table 9).

- Lake States pulpwood production for pulp mills during 2000-2004 is shown in table A on the top of this page.

Michigan

- Michigan produced 2.2 million cords of wood material for wood pulp in 2004, an increase of 4 percent from 2003 (fig. 13).

- Aspen, soft maple, and hard maple were the major pulpwood species groups harvested in the State in 2004. All together, these three species groups accounted for more than 60 percent of the total roundwood harvested.

- Michigan wood pulp mills imported 242 thousand cords of pulpwood, mostly from Wisconsin. Michigan exported almost 380 thousand cords to wood pulp mills in Minnesota, Wisconsin, and Canada.

Figure 13.— *Pulpwood production in the Lake States for pulp by State, 2003-2004.*

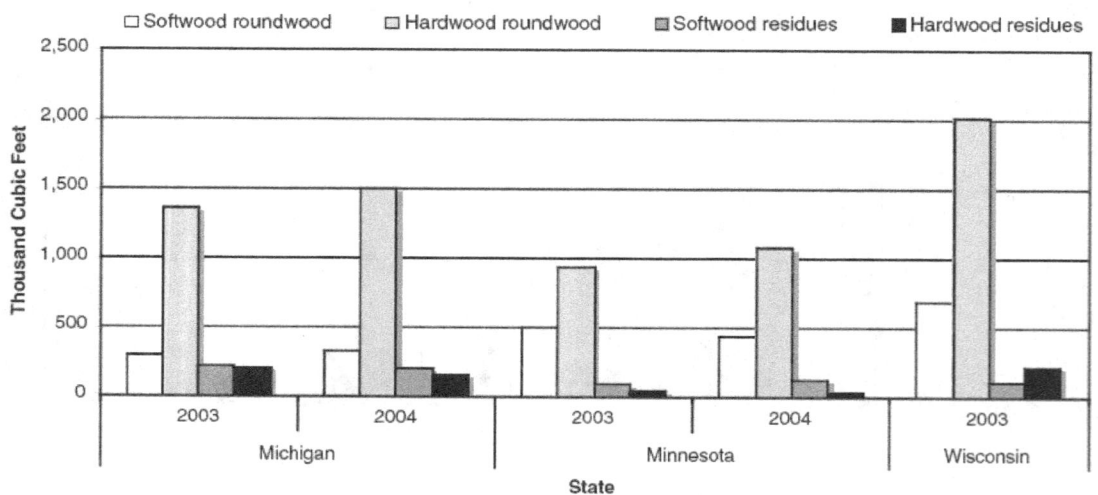

Minnesota

- Pulpwood production for wood pulp totaled 1.7 million cords in 2004, an increase of almost 8 percent from 2003.

- In 2004, aspen remained the predominant species harvested in the State with 756 thousand cords or almost half of the total roundwood produced. Other major species harvested were spruce with 163 thousand cords and balsam fir with 160 thousand cords.

- Pulp mills in Minnesota imported 537 thousand cords of wood material from Michigan, Wisconsin, and Canada. Minnesota exported 117 thousand cords to pulp mills in Wisconsin and Canada.

Wisconsin

- Pulpwood production for wood pulp products increased by 6 percent to 3.2 million cords in 2004.

- Aspen was the main species harvested with 627 thousand cords. Other major species harvested were hard maple (458 thousand cords), soft maple (409 thousand cords), white birch (273 thousand cords), and red pine (221 thousand cords).

- Wisconsin mills imported 454 thousand cords of pulpwood: 303 thousand cords from Michigan, 93 thousand cords from Minnesota, 3 thousand cords from other States, and 55 thousand cords from Canada. Wisconsin exported 327 thousand cords to Minnesota, 212 thousand cords to Michigan, and 4 thousand cords to other States.

Particleboard Mill

Particleboard is a generic term for a panel manufactured from lignocellulosic material—commonly wood—essentially in the form of particles (as distinct from fibers). These materials are bonded together with synthetic resin or other suitable binder under heat and pressure by a process wherein the inter-particle bonds are created wholly by the added binder. Other materials may have been added during manufacture to improve certain properties. The many types of particleboard differ greatly in the size and geometry of the particle, the amount of resin (adhesive) used, and the density to which the panel is pressed. Products included in the particleboard group include particleboard, waferboard, oriented strandboard (OSB), and engineered lumber. The major types of particles used for particleboard are shavings, flakes, wafers, chips, sawdust, strands, slivers, and wood wool (excelsior). Much of the particleboard in the U.S. is made from residues (shavings, sawdust, or chips). Waferboard, OSB, and engineered lumber are examples of products requiring that the particles be cut from solid wood (saw logs or pulpwood). Wood material from the Lake States sent to mills in other States and Canada is included.

- The Lake States produced 2.7 million cords of pulpwood in 2004 for particleboard products, down by 2 percent from 2003 (fig. 14).

- Twelve of the fifteen Lake States mills in the particleboard category were OSB or engineered wood product mills that require particles to be cut from roundwood. Hence, for every cord of pulpwood used in particleboard manufacture, 94 percent came from roundwood.

- Principal species harvested for particleboard products were aspen (1.8 million cords), jack pine (233 thousand cords), white birch (128 thousand cords), and soft maple (103 thousand cords).

Figure 14.—*Pulpwood production for particleboard in the Lake States, 2000-2004.*

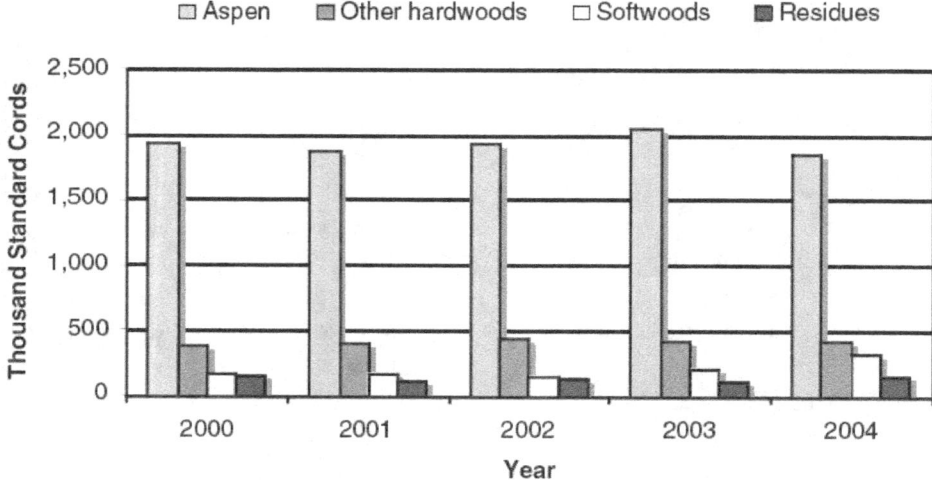

- In 2004, the Lake States produced 316 thousand cords of softwood roundwood and 2.3 million cords of hardwood roundwood for processing at particleboard plants. Less than 1 percent of the roundwood harvested in the Lake States for particleboard production was exported to other States.

- The Lake States in 2004 produced 80 thousand cords of softwood residues and 75 thousand cords of hardwood residues for use in particleboard production. Between 2003 and 2004, the use of residues for particleboard production increased by more than 35 percent.

- Annual production at Lake States particleboard plants fell from 2,125 million square feet 3/4-inch basis in 2003 to 2,064 million square feet 3/4-inch basis in 2004 (table 10).

- Lake States pulpwood production for particleboard mills during 2000-2004 is shown in table B.

Michigan

- The production of wood material for particleboard production in Michigan increased by 3 percent from 2003 to 2004, rising from 891 thousand cords in 2003 to 918 thousand cords in 2004 (fig. 15).

- In 2004, the harvest of roundwood from Michigan forest land provided 823 thousand cords of wood for particleboard products, of which almost 80 percent were hardwoods. Residues from Michigan's primary wood-using mills provided another 95 thousand cords of wood material used to produce particleboard products.

Table B.—*Lake States pulpwood production for particleboard mills during 2000-2004*

Product form and species	Production				
	2000	2001	2002	2003	2004
	- - - - - - - - - - - - - - - - (Thousand cords) - - - - - - - - - - - - - - - -				
Roundwood					
Softwoods	160	174	149	204	316
Aspen	1,939	1,880	1,938	2,058	1,849
Other hardwoods	374	396	431	426	426
Residues	156	108	129	113	156
Total	2,628	2,558	2,647	2,801	2,747

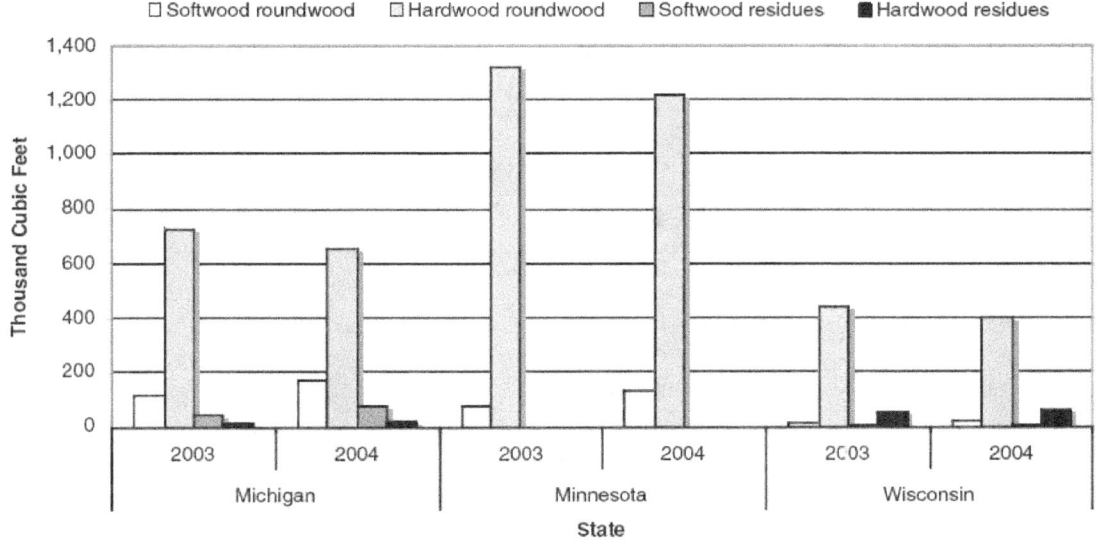

Figure 15.—
Pulpwood pro-
duction in the
Lake States for
particleboard by
State, 2003-
2004.

- The particleboard mills in Michigan imported 71 thousand cords from Canada and 56 thousand cords from Wisconsin. Almost 35 thousand cords of wood material for particleboard production were exported to Minnesota, Wisconsin, States outside the North-Central Region, and to Canada.

Minnesota

- The production of roundwood for particleboard production in Minnesota decreased by 3 percent, from 1.4 million cords in 2003 to 1.3 million cords in 2004. In 2004, there were no residues from primary wood-using mills in Minnesota that were used in particleboard mills.

- Minnesota accounted for nearly half of all the wood material produced in the Lake States for particleboard plants in 2004. Aspen was the predominant species harvested (1.0 million cords) for particleboard production. White birch, at 102 thousand cords, was the second most important species harvested.

- The particleboard mills in Minnesota imported 123 thousand cords from Canada and almost 23 thousand cords from North Dakota, Wisconsin, and Michigan combined. In 2004,

raw materials exported from the State for particleboard manufacturing totaled 67 thousand cords, all of which went to Wisconsin.

Wisconsin

- The production of wood material for particleboard production in Wisconsin decreased by 7 percent, falling from 516 thousand cords in 2003 to 479 thousand cords in 2004.

- In 2004, there was 418 thousand cords of roundwood harvested from Wisconsin forest land for particleboard manufacturing, of which 17 thousand cords were softwood and 401 thousand cords were hardwood. Wisconsin's primary wood-processing mills provided an additional 61 thousand cords of plant byproducts to the particleboard industry.

- The mills in Wisconsin imported almost 110 thousand cords of wood for particleboard manufacturing: 67 thousand cords from Minnesota, 35 thousand cords from Canada, and 8 thousand cords from Michigan. Wisconsin exported 56 thousand cords to Michigan particleboard mills and 6 thousand cords to Minnesota particleboard mills in 2004.

CENTRAL STATES

PRODUCTION

Because of the limited number of pulp mills in the Central States, detailed county information is not reported to avoid disclosure of individual mill receipts.

- Pulpwood production in the Central States (Illinois, Indiana, Iowa, and Missouri) increased by 5 percent, from 462 thousand cords in 2003 to 484 thousand cords in 2004.

- Pulpwood production from roundwood harvested in the Central States increased by 10 percent, and pulpwood production from residues from primary wood-processing mills in the Central States increased by 2 percent.

- Wood residues accounted for almost two-thirds of the total wood material produced in the Central States for the pulp and particleboard industry in 2004 (table 11).

- Pulpwood production from softwood roundwood decreased by almost 30 percent from 2003 to 2004, soft hardwood[6] roundwood production decreased by 3 percent, and hard hardwood[7] production increased by 16 percent (table 12 and fig. 16).

- Exports of roundwood and residues from the Central States in 2004 accounted for 78 percent of all wood material produced in the region for pulpwood production. Roundwood exports totaled 166 thousand cords, and the export of residues from primary wood-processing mills totaled 318 thousand cords.

- Loggers harvested pulpwood in 13 counties in Illinois, 16 counties in Indiana, 2 counties in Iowa, and 11 counties in Missouri.

- Pulpwood production from whole-tree chips increased by 8 percent between 2003 and 2004. The 30 thousand cords of whole-tree chips made up 18 percent of the total roundwood produced in the Central States in 2004.

---

6 Hardwood species with an average specific gravity of 0.50 or less.

7 Hardwood species with an average specific gravity greater than 0.50.

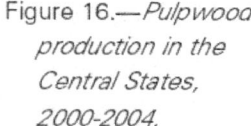

Figure 16.—*Pulpwood production in the Central States, 2000-2004.*

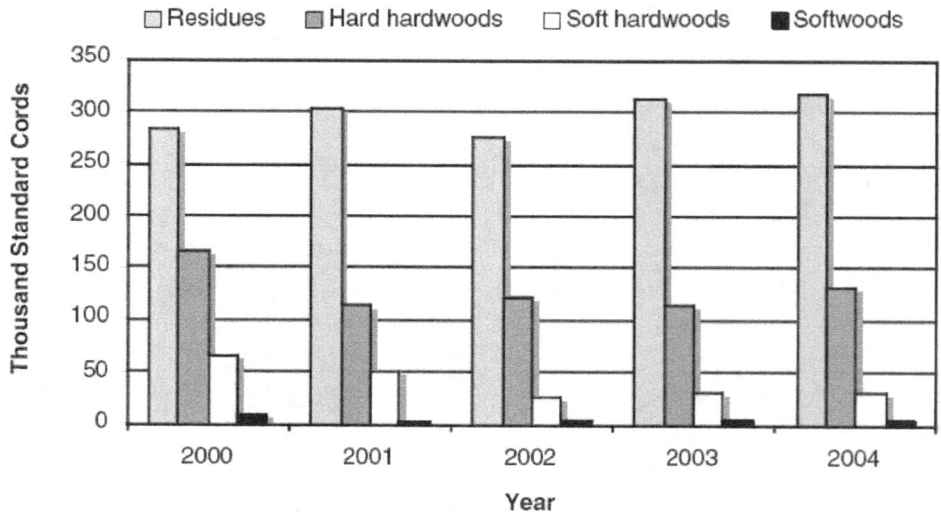

Illinois

- Illinois does not have any primary wood pulp or particleboard mills; consequently, all pulpwood harvested and residues produced by primary wood-processing mills, which are utilized by pulp or particleboard mills, are shipped to plants outside the State.

- Illinois produced 38 thousand cords of pulpwood in 2004, a decrease of more than 13 percent from the previous year (fig. 17 and table 13).

- Illinois supplied 14 percent of the Central States total roundwood produced in 2004. Pulpwood production from residues accounted for 5 percent of the Central States total residue production. Overall, Illinois contributed almost 10 percent of the total pulpwood produced in the Central States.

Indiana

- Pulpwood production increased by 3 percent in Indiana, from 154 thousand cords in 2003 to 159 thousand cords in 2004. Indiana produced almost one-third of the total pulpwood produced in the Central States in 2004.

- Roundwood production increased by almost 16 percent from 2003 to 2004, while residue production increased by only 1 percent.

Iowa

- The total pulpwood produced in Iowa in 2004 was 25 thousand cords, the same as in 2003. The State contributed 5 percent of the total pulpwood produced in the Central States.

- The production of wood material for pulping remained at 2003 levels of 5 thousand cords of roundwood and 20 thousand cords of residues from primary wood processors.

Missouri

- Missouri remained the largest producer of pulpwood in the Central States in 2004 with 52 percent of the regional total or 262 thousand cords. The production of pulpwood in Missouri increased by almost 10 percent between 2003 and 2004.

- Missouri produced 111 thousand cords of roundwood and 151 thousand cords of residues for pulpwood in 2004.

- Missouri exported almost 93 percent of its pulpwood production to mills in the Southern States.

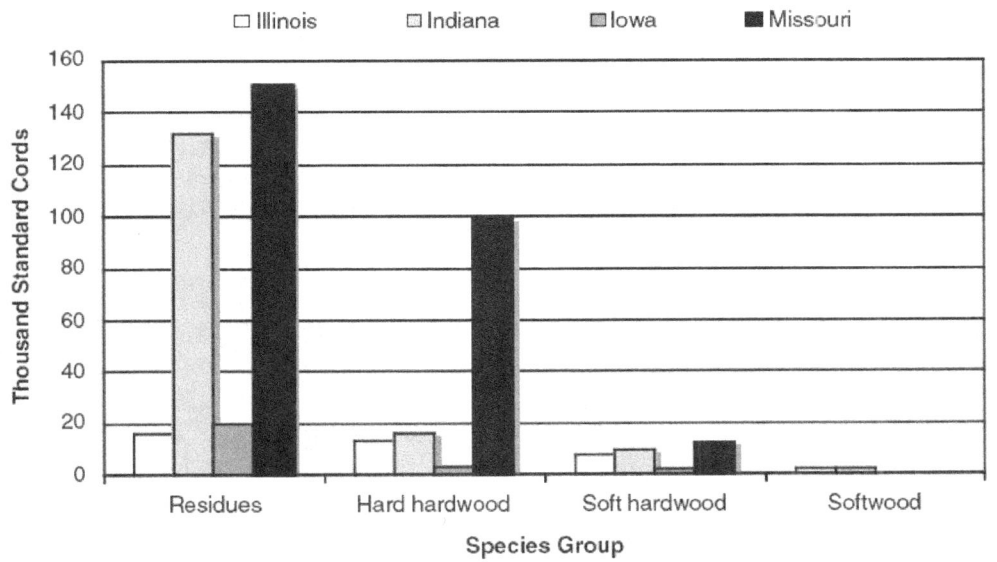

Figure 17.—Central States pulpwood production by State, species group, and residues, 2004.

RECEIPTS

Because of the limited number of pulp mills in the Central States, State receipts are not reported to avoid disclosure of individual mill receipts.

- Pulp mills in the Central States received 139 thousand cords in 2004, an increase of 29 percent from 2003.

- Roundwood receipts increased by 8 percent, from 29 thousand cords in 2003 to 31 thousand cords in 2004. Residue receipts increased by more than 36 percent, from 79 thousand cords in 2003 to 108 thousand cords in 2004.

INDUSTRY TRENDS AND ANALYSIS

- Average daily wood pulp production for pulp mills in the Central States between 2003 and 2004 increased to 564 tons, an increase of only 1 ton (table 14).

- In 2004, only 19 percent of the roundwood and 34 percent of the residues produced for pulpwood in the Central States went to pulp mills located in the Central States.

- Hardwood residues from sawmills and other wood-using mills accounted for 71 percent of all the wood material used by the Central States pulp mills. It continues to be the dominant form of wood material procured.

PLAINS STATES

Because of the limited number of pulp mills in the Plains States, detailed production and receipts are not reported to avoid disclosure of individual mill receipts.

PRODUCTION

- In 2004, the Plains States produced 116 thousand cords of roundwood and mill residues for pulpwood production, an increase of more than 80 percent from 2003 (fig. 18). Pulpwood came from Kansas, North Dakota, and South Dakota.

- Softwood residues accounted for more than two-thirds of the pulpwood production for the Plains States in 2004 (fig. 19).

- The only species harvested from the Plains States for pulpwood production in 2004 were ponderosa pine, aspen, balsam poplar, and cottonwood.

- The only mill in the Plains States in 2004 was Merillat Industries, Inc. (particleboard), in Rapid City, SD, which has an annual production capacity of 93 million square feet 3/4-inch basis.

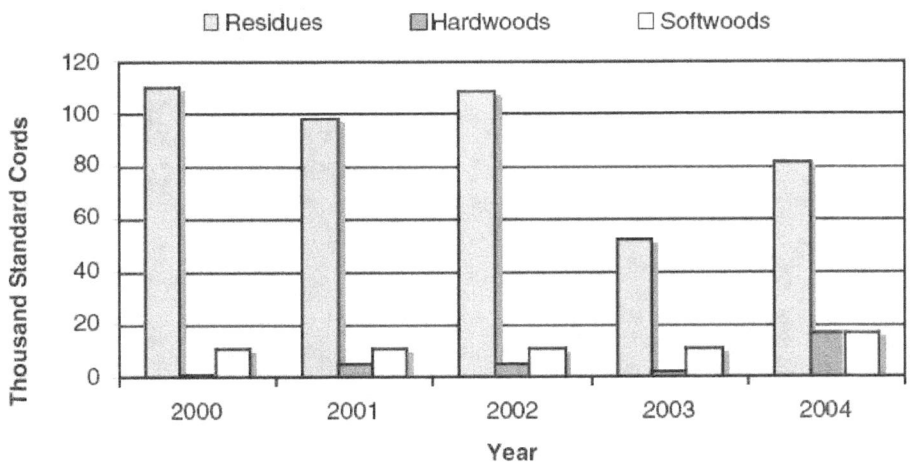

Figure 18.— *Pulpwood production in the Plains States, 2000-2004.*

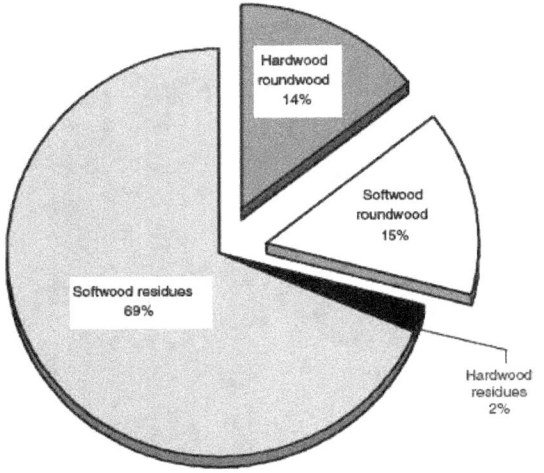

Figure 19.— *Plains States pulpwood production by species group and residues, 2004.*

19

APPENDIX

CONVERSION FACTORS USED IN THE NORTH-CENTRAL REGION

Standard cords of green roundwood per green ton:

Species	Factor	Species	Factor
Softwoods	0.4688	White birch	0.4018
Northern white-cedar	.6329	Yellow birch	.3723
Balsam fir	.4688	River birch	.3871
Hemlock	.4150	Sweetgum	.3669
Jack pine	.4688	Yellow-poplar	.4219
Red pine	.4688	Blackgum	.3779
White pine	.4777	Sycamore	.4083
Shortleaf pine	.3956	Cottonwood	.4291
Spruce	.5014	Elm	.4018
Tamarack	.4291	Hickory	.3701
Hardwoods	.3939	Hard maple	.3617
Soft hardwoods	.4171	Soft maple	.4083
Hard hardwoods	.3708	Black cherry	.4688
Ash	.4330	Red oak	.3444
Aspen	.4291	White oak	.3723
Balsam poplar	.4083	Black oak	.3444
Basswood	.5167	Other hardwoods	.4777
Beech	.3956		

TABLE TITLES

Table 1.—*Production and imports of pulpwood, Lake States, 2004*

Table 2.—*Lake States pulpwood production by State of origin, year, and destination, 2000-2004*

Table 3.—*Lake States pulpwood production from roundwood by State, Forest Survey Unit, and species group, 2000-2004*

Table 4.—*Lake States pulpwood production by State of origin, product form, Forest Survey Unit, and destination, 2004*

Table 5.—*Pulpwood production from roundwood by Forest Survey Unit, county, and species group, Michigan, 2004*

Table 6.—*Pulpwood production from roundwood by Forest Survey Unit, county, and species group, Minnesota, 2004*

Table 7.—*Pulpwood production from roundwood by Forest Survey Unit, county, and species group, Wisconsin, 2004*

Table 8.—*Number of industrial pulp or particleboard plants in the Lake States by product form, species group used, and State, 2004*

Table 9.—*Average daily production of active wood pulp mills in the Lake States by State, company, location, and type of pulp produced, 2004*

Table 10.—*Annual production of active particleboard and panel mills in the Lake States by State, company, location, and product produced, 2004*

Table 11.—*Production and imports of pulpwood, Central States, 2004*

Table 12.—*Central States pulpwood production by product form and species group, 2000-2004*

Table 13.— *Central States pulpwood production by State and destination, 2000-2004*

Table 14.—*Average daily production of active wood pulp mills in the Central States by company, location, and type of pulp produced, 2004*

RB-NC-265 continues on next page

TABLES

Table 1.--Production and imports of pulpwood, Lake States, 2004

(In standard cords, unpeeled)

Product form, species group, and destination	Production by State[1]				Imports				Total receipts
	Michigan	Minnesota	Wisconsin	Regional total	Central States	Plains States	Canada	Total imports	
Softwood roundwood									
Northern white-cedar									
Michigan	4,245	--	46	4,291	--	--	--	--	4,291
Minnesota	--	214	--	214	--	--	--	--	214
Total	4,245	214	46	4,505	--	--	--	--	4,505
Balsam fir									
Canada	8,039	--	--	8,039	--	--	--	--	--
Michigan	65,959	--	737	66,696	--	--	--	--	66,696
Minnesota	148	166,882	24,032	191,062	--	--	1,358	1,358	192,420
Wisconsin	5,167	181	52,995	58,344	--	--	40	40	58,383
Total	79,314	167,063	77,764	324,141	--	--	1,398	1,398	317,500
Hemlock									
Michigan	62,193	--	4,409	66,602	--	--	--	--	66,602
Wisconsin	949	--	25,177	26,126	--	--	--	--	26,126
Total	63,141	--	29,586	92,727	--	--	--	--	92,727
Jack pine									
Canada	--	590	--	590	--	--	--	--	--
Michigan	196,779	--	937	197,716	--	--	--	--	197,716
Minnesota	--	152,915	5,510	158,426	--	--	591	591	159,016
Other[2]	576	--	--	576	--	--	--	--	--
Wisconsin	1,434	2,379	155,635	159,448	280	--	80	361	159,809
Total	198,788	155,884	162,082	516,755	280	--	671	952	516,541
Red pine									
Canada	--	380	--	380	--	--	--	--	--
Michigan	48,213	--	1,483	49,695	--	--	--	--	49,695
Minnesota	--	43,257	4,615	47,872	--	--	--	--	47,872
Other[2]	142	--	--	142	--	--	--	--	--
Wisconsin	2,553	2,809	218,845	224,207	656	--	--	656	224,863
Total	50,907	46,446	224,942	322,296	656	--	--	656	322,431
White pine									
Canada	--	380	--	380	--	--	--	--	--
Michigan	7,663	--	193	7,856	--	--	--	--	7,856
Minnesota	--	1,941	295	2,236	--	--	453	453	2,688
Other[2]	29	--	--	29	--	--	--	--	--
Wisconsin	894	81	57,809	58,785	136	--	523	659	59,443
Total	8,587	2,402	58,297	69,285	136	--	976	1,111	69,988
Spruce									
Canada	8,792	--	--	8,792	--	--	--	--	--
Michigan	26,428	--	352	26,781	--	--	--	--	26,781
Minnesota	163	146,193	3,280	149,636	--	--	4,813	4,813	154,449
Wisconsin	38,761	18,354	54,342	111,457	--	--	10,117	10,117	121,574
Total	74,144	164,547	57,974	296,666	--	--	14,930	14,930	302,804

Tamarack								
Michigan	13,598	--	162	13,760	--	--	--	13,760
Minnesota	--	27,455	104	27,559	--	258	258	27,817
Wisconsin	5,645	12,204	16,130	33,979	--	2,400	2,400	36,379
Total	19,242	39,659	16,396	75,297	--	2,658	2,658	77,955
Other softwoods								
Michigan	5,498	--	--	5,498	--	--	--	5,498
Minnesota	--	80	49	129	--	--	--	129
Total	5,498	80	49	5,627	--	--	--	5,627
Total softwood roundwood								
Canada	16,831	1,349	--	18,180	--	--	--	--
Michigan	430,576	--	8,319	438,895	--	--	--	438,895
Minnesota	311	538,937	37,886	577,133	--	7,473	7,473	584,606
Other[2]	746	--	--	746	--	--	--	--
Wisconsin	55,403	36,008	580,933	672,345	1,072	13,160	14,232	686,577
Total	503,868	576,294	627,138	1,707,299	1,072	20,633	21,705	1,710,078
Softwood residues								
Canada	23,110	21,348	--	44,458	--	--	--	--
Michigan	163,094	--	15	163,109	--	455	455	163,109
Minnesota	--	102,358	1,704	104,062	--	--	--	104,517
Wisconsin	90,058	1,575	107,242	198,875	--	14,442	14,442	213,317
Total	276,262	125,281	108,961	510,504	--	14,897	14,897	480,943
Total softwood material								
Canada	39,941	22,697	--	62,638	--	--	--	--
Michigan	593,670	--	8,333	602,003	--	--	--	602,003
Minnesota	311	641,295	39,590	681,195	--	7,928	7,928	689,123
Other[2]	746	--	--	746	--	--	--	--
Wisconsin	145,461	37,583	688,175	871,220	1,072	27,602	28,674	899,894
Total	780,130	701,575	736,098	2,217,803	1,072	35,530	36,603	2,191,021

(Table 1 continued on next page)

(Table 1 continued)

26

Product form, species group, and destination	Production by State[1]				Imports				Total receipts
	Michigan	Minnesota	Wisconsin	Regional total	Central States	Plains States	Canada	Total imports	
Hardwood roundwood									
Ash									
Michigan	26,342	--	4,470	30,813	--	--	416	416	31,228
Minnesota	1,352	17,382	5,968	24,702	--	--	2,370	2,370	27,072
Wisconsin	8,113	51	79,397	87,561	--	--	1,104	1,104	88,665
Total	35,808	17,433	89,835	143,075	--	--	3,890	3,890	146,965
Aspen									
Michigan	792,194	--	43,133	835,327	--	--	71,044	71,044	906,371
Minnesota	6,281	1,728,170	116,099	1,850,550	--	16,114	211,867	227,981	2,078,531
Other[2]	557	--	--	557	--	--	--	--	--
Wisconsin	47,348	66,241	816,928	930,517	--	--	34,749	34,749	965,266
Total	846,379	1,794,411	976,161	3,616,950	--	16,114	317,660	333,774	3,950,168
Balsam poplar									
Michigan	47,416	--	4,723	52,139	--	--	635	635	52,775
Minnesota	165	119,225	2,677	122,068	--	54	13,119	13,173	135,240
Wisconsin	--	--	--	--	--	--	290	290	290
Total	47,581	119,225	7,400	174,207	--	54	14,044	14,098	188,305
Basswood									
Michigan	56,246	--	15,067	71,313	--	--	744	744	72,057
Minnesota	1,951	24,455	11,232	37,638	--	--	2,656	2,656	40,294
Other[2]	45	--	--	45	--	--	--	--	--
Wisconsin	4,967	200	70,972	76,139	--	--	--	--	76,139
Total	63,210	24,655	97,271	185,136	--	--	3,400	3,400	188,491
Beech									
Michigan	52,888	--	11,182	64,069	--	--	1,139	1,139	65,209
Other[2]	6	--	--	6	--	--	--	--	--
Wisconsin	147	--	86,213	86,360	--	--	--	--	86,360
Total	53,041	--	97,394	150,436	--	--	1,139	1,139	151,569
White birch									
Michigan	83,618	--	11,909	95,527	--	--	1,157	1,157	96,684
Minnesota	1,514	197,337	18,261	217,113	--	--	5,288	5,288	222,401
Other[2]	26	--	--	26	--	--	--	--	--
Wisconsin	25,133	42,847	248,738	316,718	--	--	6,313	6,313	323,030
Total	110,291	240,185	278,908	629,384	--	--	12,758	12,758	642,116
Yellow birch									
Michigan	33,652	--	9,154	42,805	--	--	894	894	43,699
Wisconsin	3,730	--	28,139	31,870	--	--	--	--	31,870
Total	37,382	--	37,293	74,675	--	--	894	894	75,569
Cottonwood									
Minnesota	--	577	10	587	--	626	--	626	1,212
Total	--	577	10	587	--	626	--	626	1,212
Elm									
Michigan	1,862	--	--	1,862	--	--	--	--	1,862
Minnesota	1,093	1,405	2,866	5,364	--	--	390	390	5,754
Wisconsin	2,440	--	15,653	18,092	--	--	--	--	18,092
Total	5,394	1,405	18,519	25,318	--	--	390	390	25,708

Hickory							
Michigan	3,130	--	--	3,130	--	--	3,130
Wisconsin	125	--	1,233	1,358	--	--	1,358
Total	3,255	--	1,233	4,489	--	--	4,489
Hard maple							
Michigan	325,467	--	67,381	392,848	6,424	6,424	399,272
Minnesota	33,203	25,864	61,196	120,263	11,991	11,991	132,254
Wisconsin	29,447	5,897	334,513	369,857	6,620	6,620	376,477
Total	388,117	31,762	463,090	882,968	25,035	25,035	908,003
Soft maple							
Michigan	404,576	--	70,375	474,951	7,055	7,055	482,007
Minnesota	12,494	66,603	68,339	147,436	4,455	4,455	151,891
Other	146	--	--	146	--	--	--
Wisconsin	31,984	580	281,923	314,487	5,516	5,516	320,003
Total	449,199	67,183	420,637	937,020	17,026	17,026	953,900
Red oak							
Michigan	57,699	--	5,199	62,898	496	496	63,394
Minnesota	--	192	13	205	--	--	205
Wisconsin	2,756	261	133,719	136,737	5,516	5,516	142,253
Total	60,455	453	138,931	199,840	6,012	6,012	205,851
White oak							
Michigan	27,614	--	--	27,614	--	--	27,614
Minnesota	--	233	14	246	--	--	246
Wisconsin	1,099	106	35,371	36,576	2,206	2,206	38,782
Total	28,713	339	35,385	64,436	2,206	2,206	66,643
Other hardwoods							
Michigan	23,609	--	4,522	28,132	459	459	28,590
Minnesota	1,299	1,670	3,408	6,377	463	463	6,841
Wisconsin	448	--	5,005	5,453	--	--	5,453
Total	25,357	1,670	12,936	39,962	922	922	40,884

(Table 1 continued on next page)

(Table 1 continued)

Product form, species group, and destination	Production by State [1]			Regional total	Imports			Total imports	Total receipts
	Michigan	Minnesota	Wisconsin		Central States	Plains States	Canada		
Total hardwood roundwood									
Michigan	1,936,312	--	247,116	2,183,428	--	--	90,463	90,463	2,273,891
Minnesota	59,352	2,183,114	290,083	2,532,548	--	16,794	252,599	269,392	2,801,941
Other⁴	780	--	--	780	--	--	--	--	--
Wisconsin	157,738	116,185	2,137,804	2,411,726	--	--	62,314	62,314	2,474,040
Total	2,154,181	2,299,298	2,675,003	7,128,483	--	16,794	405,376	422,169	7,549,872
Hardwood residues									
Canada	2,008	1,720	--	3,728	--	--	--	--	--
Michigan	160,826	--	12,138	172,964	10,594	--	--	10,594	183,558
Minnesota	38	26,023	2,618	28,679	--	--	13,167	13,167	41,846
Other²	--	--	3,833	3,833	--	--	--	--	--
Wisconsin	7,832	5,820	254,406	268,058	1,778	--	--	1,778	269,836
Total	170,704	33,564	272,995	477,262	12,372	--	13,167	25,539	495,240
Total hardwood material									
Canada	2,008	1,720	--	3,728	--	--	--	--	--
Michigan	2,097,138	--	259,255	2,356,393	10,594	--	90,463	101,057	2,457,449
Minnesota	59,390	2,209,137	292,701	2,561,227	--	16,794	265,766	282,559	2,843,787
Other²	780	--	3,833	4,613	--	--	--	--	--
Wisconsin	165,570	122,005	2,392,210	2,679,785	1,778	--	62,314	64,092	2,743,876
Total	2,324,885	2,332,862	2,947,998	7,605,745	12,372	16,794	418,543	447,708	8,045,113
Total all roundwood									
Canada	16,831	1,349	--	18,180	--	--	--	--	--
Michigan	2,366,888	--	255,435	2,622,323	--	--	90,463	90,463	2,712,786
Minnesota	59,663	2,722,050	327,969	3,109,682	--	16,794	260,072	276,865	3,386,547
Other²	1,526	--	--	1,526	--	--	--	--	--
Wisconsin	213,141	152,193	2,718,737	3,084,071	1,072	--	75,474	76,546	3,160,617
Total	2,658,049	2,875,593	3,302,141	8,835,782	1,072	16,794	426,009	443,875	9,259,950
Total all residues									
Canada	25,118	23,068	--	48,186	--	--	--	--	--
Michigan	323,920	--	12,153	336,073	10,594	--	--	10,594	346,667
Minnesota	38	128,382	4,322	132,741	--	--	13,622	13,622	146,363
Other²	--	--	3,833	3,833	--	--	--	--	--
Wisconsin	97,890	7,395	361,648	466,933	1,778	--	14,442	16,220	483,153
Total	446,966	158,844	381,956	987,766	12,372	--	28,065	40,436	976,183
Total all wood material									
Canada	41,949	24,417	--	66,367	--	--	--	--	--
Michigan	2,690,808	--	267,588	2,958,396	10,594	--	90,463	101,057	3,059,453
Minnesota	59,700	2,850,432	332,290	3,242,423	--	16,794	273,694	290,488	3,532,910
Other²	1,526	--	3,833	5,359	--	--	--	--	--
Wisconsin	311,031	159,588	3,080,385	3,551,004	2,850	--	89,916	92,766	3,643,770
Total	3,105,015	3,034,437	3,684,096	9,823,548	13,444	16,794	454,073	484,311	10,236,134

[1] Vertical columns of figures under the box heading "Production by State" present the amount of roundwood cut or residue generated in each State.

² Pulpwood shipped to mills outside of region.

Table may not add due to rounding.

Table 2.--Lake States pulpwood production by State of origin, year, and destination, 2000-2004

(In thousand standard cords, unpeeled) [1]

MICHIGAN

Year	Total production	Destination of pulpwood			
		Michigan	Minnesota	Wisconsin	Other[2]
2000	3,140	2,834	7	272	27
2001	2,898	2,570	9	299	20
2002	2,900	2,615	10	254	21
2003	2,987	2,689	26	247	25
2004	3,105	2,691	60	311	43
5-year average	3,006	2,680	22	277	27

MINNESOTA

Year	Total production	Destination of pulpwood			
		Michigan	Minnesota	Wisconsin	Other[2]
2000	3,036	--	2,803	211	21
2001	2,839	--	2,630	187	22
2002	3,015	--	2,865	139	11
2003	2,958	--	2,757	191	10
2004	3,035	--	2,851	160	24
5-year average	2,977	--	2,781	178	18

WISCONSIN

Year	Total production	Destination of pulpwood			
		Michigan	Minnesota	Wisconsin	Other[2]
2000	3,420	195	151	3,068	6
2001	3,309	274	133	2,898	4
2002	3,485	256	360	2,864	6
2003	3,549	275	355	2,915	4
2004	3,684	268	332	3,080	4
5-year average	3,489	254	266	2,965	5

[1] Includes mill residues used for pulp.

[2] Includes other States and Canada.
Table may not add due to rounding.

Table 3.--Lake States pulpwood production from roundwood by State, Forest Survey Unit, and species group, 2000-2004

(In thousand standard cords, unpeeled)

Forest Survey Unit	All species					Pine					Spruce				
	2000	2001	2002	2003	2004	2000	2001	2002	2003	2004	2000	2001	2002	2003	2004
MICHIGAN															
Eastern Upper Peninsula	575	646	629	603	594	110	117	69	56	58	19	26	19	18	22
Western Upper Peninsula	1,141	959	933	953	1,035	66	59	46	40	46	30	32	27	27	46
Northern Lower Peninsula	884	789	829	874	951	106	106	74	100	150	3	2	1	4	6
Southern Lower Peninsula	76	53	61	68	78	1	1	2	2	4	0	--	--	--	0
Total	2,676	2,446	2,451	2,497	2,658	283	284	192	198	258	51	61	47	49	74
MINNESOTA															
Aspen-Birch	1,210	1,171	1,233	1,179	1,316	44	59	60	43	74	125	148	145	150	124
Northern Pine	1,428	1,318	1,373	1,350	1,295	62	63	88	75	118	56	51	69	67	40
Central Hardwoods	228	180	210	217	209	10	15	14	10	12	1	1	1	1	1
Prairie	71	86	91	84	56	0	0	0	1	1	0	0	0	0	0
Total	2,937	2,755	2,907	2,830	2,876	116	138	163	128	205	182	200	215	218	165
WISCONSIN															
Northeastern	1,002	1,001	994	1,079	1,167	146	115	88	109	84	31	24	19	26	26
Northwestern	1,211	1,159	1,340	1,311	1,309	190	168	134	103	90	28	15	25	30	26
Central	650	645	634	681	729	262	270	251	261	232	4	6	3	5	3
Southwestern	87	78	80	61	54	44	31	29	32	24	2	2	1	2	2
Southeastern	25	50	39	42	44	13	15	19	19	15	2	2	1	2	1
Total	2,974	2,932	3,087	3,174	3,302	655	600	521	524	445	66	49	49	65	58
Total Lake States	8,588	8,133	8,446	8,501	8,836	1,054	1,021	875	850	810	300	309	311	332	297

(Table 3 continued on next page)

(Table 3 continued)

MICHIGAN

Forest Survey Unit	Balsam fir 2000	2001	2002	2003	2004	Other softwoods 2000	2001	2002	2003	2004	Aspen 2000	2001	2002	2003	2004
Eastern Upper Peninsula	23	26	33	26	35	24	40	32	33	33	144	153	160	149	134
Western Upper Peninsula	36	33	33	33	37	65	62	51	55	50	308	292	269	286	290
Northern Lower Peninsula	6	4	4	7	7	0	0	0	4	9	380	366	388	410	403
Southern Lower Peninsula	--	--	0	--	0	--	--	--	--	0	19	15	15	18	19
Total	64	64	70	66	79	90	103	84	91	92	850	826	832	863	846

MINNESOTA

Forest Survey Unit	Balsam fir 2000	2001	2002	2003	2004	Other softwoods 2000	2001	2002	2003	2004	Aspen 2000	2001	2002	2003	2004
Aspen-Birch	110	101	94	93	117	12	25	20	37	22	780	699	754	632	723
Northern Pine	72	68	74	74	48	6	21	7	21	17	1,091	968	970	921	874
Central Hardwoods	2	1	1	1	2	0	0	0	0	1	194	147	156	168	146
Prairie	--	0	0	0	0	0	0	0	0	--	69	82	84	75	52
Total	184	171	169	168	167	18	46	28	59	40	2,134	1,895	1,965	1,796	1,794

WISCONSIN

Forest Survey Unit	Balsam fir 2000	2001	2002	2003	2004	Other softwoods 2000	2001	2002	2003	2004	Aspen 2000	2001	2002	2003	2004
Northeastern	40	35	31	25	32	25	24	22	31	29	343	291	290	320	343
Northwestern	42	48	39	45	44	10	7	13	10	12	507	415	546	479	440
Central	1	1	1	1	2	2	2	4	3	4	147	137	145	172	177
Southwestern	4	0	--	0	0	--	0	2	--	0	12	12	11	9	10
Southeastern	--	0	0	0	0	0	0	0	1	1	3	10	5	7	7
Total	87	84	71	71	78	37	33	40	46	46	1,012	865	996	987	976
Total Lake States	335	319	311	306	324	144	182	152	196	178	3,996	3,586	3,793	3,646	3,617

(Table 3 continued on next page)

31

(Table 3 continued)

MICHIGAN

Forest Survey Unit	White and yellow birches					Hard and soft maples					Other hardwoods				
	2000	2001	2002	2003	2004	2000	2001	2002	2003	2004	2000	2001	2002	2003	2004
Eastern Upper Peninsula	47	43	45	45	42	170	194	212	211	207	40	46	58	65	63
Western Upper Peninsula	110	68	71	73	76	415	308	340	339	374	112	104	95	100	116
Northern Lower Peninsula	43	31	28	25	29	219	196	239	222	234	127	83	95	102	112
Southern Lower Peninsula	1	0	1	1	1	26	16	19	22	23	28	20	23	25	32
Total	200	142	144	144	148	830	714	810	794	837	308	253	272	291	323

MINNESOTA

	White and yellow birches					Hard and soft maples					Other hardwoods				
	2000	2001	2002	2003	2004	2000	2001	2002	2003	2004	2000	2001	2002	2003	2004
Aspen-Birch	72	70	77	112	123	19	24	33	46	49	48	45	51	66	83
Northern Pine	73	71	77	91	94	16	18	25	34	32	51	58	62	69	72
Central Hardwoods	9	7	11	16	22	10	8	14	13	17	3	2	11	7	7
Prairie	0	0	1	1	1	--	--	0	0	0	2	4	6	7	3
Total	154	148	166	219	240	45	50	72	93	99	104	109	130	149	166

WISCONSIN

	White and yellow birches					Hard and soft maples					Other hardwoods				
	2000	2001	2002	2003	2004	2000	2001	2002	2003	2004	2000	2001	2002	2003	2004
Northeastern	89	91	95	100	123	212	287	332	340	381	117	132	118	129	149
Northwestern	133	110	119	128	162	207	258	333	361	376	94	138	131	155	161
Central	30	28	27	32	27	75	90	101	110	113	128	111	102	98	171
Southwestern	3	3	8	2	3	11	20	20	9	8	11	10	10	7	8
Southeastern	1	3	2	2	2	4	12	7	7	7	3	8	5	4	10
Total	257	235	251	264	316	509	666	793	826	884	351	400	366	392	499
Total Lake States	611	525	561	626	704	1,384	1,430	1,675	1,713	1,820	763	761	768	832	987

0 = Less than 500 standard cords.
Table may not add due to rounding.

Table 4. -- Lake States pulpwood production by State of origin, product form, Forest Survey Unit, and destination, 2004

(In thousand standard cords, unpeeled)

MICHIGAN

Product form and Forest Survey Unit	Total production	Destination of pulpwood			
		Michigan	Minnesota	Wisconsin	Other[1]
Roundwood					
Eastern Upper Peninsula	594	519	4	62	10
Western Upper Peninsula	1,035	831	56	145	2
Northern Lower Peninsula	951	939	--	6	6
Southern Lower Peninsula	78	78	--	--	--
Total	2,658	2,367	60	213	18
Residues	447	324	0	98	25
Total pulpwood	3,105	2,691	60	311	43

MINNESOTA

Product form and Forest Survey Unit	Total production	Destination of pulpwood			
		Michigan	Minnesota	Wisconsin	Other[1]
Roundwood					
Aspen-Birch	1,316	--	1,234	80	1
Northern Pine	1,295	--	1,285	9	--
Central Hardwoods	209	--	146	63	--
Prairie	56	--	56	--	--
Total	2,876	--	2,722	152	1
Residues	159	--	128	7	23
Total pulpwood	3,034	--	2,850	160	24

WISCONSIN

Product form and Forest Survey Unit	Total production	Destination of pulpwood			
		Michigan	Minnesota	Wisconsin	Other[1]
Roundwood					
Northeastern	1,167	239	2	926	--
Northwestern	1,309	16	325	968	--
Central	729	0	0	728	--
Southwestern	54	--	1	53	--
Southeastern	44	0	0	43	--
Total	3,302	255	328	2,719	--
Residues	382	12	4	362	4
Total pulpwood	3,684	268	332	3,080	4

0 = Less than 500 standard cords, unpeeled.

[1] Includes other States and Canada.

Table may not add due to rounding.

Table 5.--Pulpwood production from roundwood by Forest Survey Unit, county, and species group, Michigan, 2004

(In standard cords, unpeeled)

Forest Survey Unit and county[1]	All species	Northern white-cedar	Balsam fir	Hemlock	Jack pine	Red pine	White pine	Spruce	Tamarack	Other softwoods	Ash	Aspen
Eastern Upper Peninsula												
Alger	76,142	293	5,590	5,234	3,086	3,205	570	2,781	2,644	--	918	9,619
Chippewa	67,163	97	3,094	2,734	3,971	2,377	126	2,795	388	--	777	19,370
Delta	80,799	382	6,184	3,824	2,608	3,699	479	3,663	1,359	--	680	20,605
Luce	96,924	155	4,367	2,185	11,319	1,321	195	2,596	553	--	1,623	18,039
Mackinac	72,897	113	2,972	886	6,109	3,326	816	2,152	381	--	582	23,117
Menominee	93,115	507	9,224	5,996	2,857	2,415	634	3,496	1,935	--	989	27,273
Schoolcraft	107,174	246	4,064	1,767	4,534	4,485	311	4,510	876	--	2,102	15,942
Total	594,213	1,792	35,494	22,627	34,485	20,828	3,132	21,992	8,137	--	7,670	133,965
Western Upper Peninsula												
Baraga	123,245	235	3,956	7,049	1,494	1,250	293	3,075	838	--	2,272	21,763
Dickinson	107,718	282	5,947	1,631	1,892	2,239	384	9,094	1,535	--	1,138	37,964
Gogebic	134,761	35	862	1,653	216	165	44	645	139	--	3,359	31,501
Houghton	101,920	75	1,252	4,722	3,941	3,740	107	1,387	266	--	2,004	31,954
Iron	137,628	427	8,813	3,168	2,904	5,578	564	17,125	1,806	--	2,030	41,845
Keweenaw	40,543	39	621	871	273	290	48	503	136	--	762	3,960
Marquette	234,396	861	13,998	16,114	10,839	6,051	1,082	12,246	3,105	--	1,798	74,039
Ontonagon	154,367	75	1,423	4,808	838	1,252	93	1,977	265	--	3,720	47,435
Total	1,034,577	2,029	36,872	40,017	22,396	20,565	2,614	46,052	8,091	--	17,082	290,460
Northern Lower Peninsula												
Alcona	37,668	22	180	--	1,924	248	127	43	--	195	156	26,717
Alpena	28,986	97	1,076	--	148	9	--	496	--	211	484	14,673
Antrim	30,442	--	--	--	5,617	99	56	--	--	767	384	8,425
Arenac	15,736	--	--	--	1,574	7	13	--	--	--	309	7,391
Bay	4,820	--	--	--	135	--	--	--	--	2	31	2,907
Benzie	21,656	--	15	--	771	95	122	2,324	--	410	671	5,405
Charlevoix	27,336	--	--	--	1,051	108	5	--	--	--	433	9,756
Cheboygan	65,986	116	2,423	--	7,567	330	57	1,286	--	372	424	36,453
Clare	36,686	--	--	--	2,971	152	20	--	--	--	396	21,362
Crawford	61,725	30	244	--	28,499	238	268	59	--	--	159	14,894
Emmet	23,728	8	60	--	203	149	1	15	--	242	200	9,293
Gladwin	29,016	--	--	--	4,339	278	37	--	--	855	126	15,596
Grand Traverse	14,076	--	--	--	2,285	532	11	--	--	--	198	4,928
Iosco	20,123	--	45	485	2,151	347	15	--	3,007	22	101	10,218
Isabella	9,541	--	--	--	97	198	--	--	--	--	108	4,821
Kalkaska	36,034	--	--	--	6,019	636	506	--	--	427	506	13,315
Lake	19,985	--	--	--	1,829	243	--	--	--	--	243	4,397
Leelanau	2,299	--	--	--	193	200	191	--	--	--	98	257
Manistee	15,229	--	--	--	510	370	51	--	--	25	533	4,751
Mason	19,730	--	--	--	746	261	--	--	--	--	527	8,741
Mecosta	16,599	--	--	--	277	143	--	--	--	--	205	9,751
Midland	27,440	--	--	--	214	40	119	--	--	--	577	11,550
Missaukee	38,891	--	--	--	3,169	359	303	--	--	--	504	18,188

County												
Montmorency	45,787	14	641	--	13,093	284	129	714	--	20	279	19,741
Newaygo	28,283	--	--	--	2,670	1,005	--	--	--	--	335	8,599
Oceana	15,102	--	--	--	1,307	87	--	--	--	--	298	5,535
Ogemaw	30,921	--	--	--	12,588	100	128	--	--	159	144	11,631
Osceola	23,733	35	--	--	509	164	--	--	--	--	443	10,883
Oscoda	27,333	--	282	--	8,700	433	71	68	--	--	59	12,236
Otsego	61,666	--	3	1	4,365	507	42	1	1	1,598	961	20,042
Presque Isle	46,761	93	1,894	2	7,136	213	114	1,074	2	24	331	24,625
Roscommon	48,055	--	--	--	10,216	674	66	--	--	--	122	21,615
Wexford	19,621	--	--	--	5,563	829	242	--	--	169	256	4,640
Total	950,991	415	6,863	489	138,436	9,339	2,695	6,079	3,009	5,498	10,602	403,336
Southern Lower Peninsula												
Allegan	11,212	--	--	--	--	--	--	--	--	--	23	1,577
Barry	1,782	--	--	--	--	--	--	--	--	--	37	729
Calhoun	2,142	--	--	--	--	--	--	--	--	--	--	242
Clinton	457	1	24	--	365	42	2	8	--	--	--	--
Gratiot	1,069	--	--	--	56	12	--	--	6	--	16	472
Huron	468	--	--	--	6	--	--	--	--	--	--	425
Ionia	2,060	--	--	--	1,238	45	--	--	--	--	6	492
Kalamazoo	7,928	--	--	--	--	--	--	--	--	--	0	897
Kent	11,116	--	--	--	305	--	143	--	--	--	97	2,330
Lapeer	29	--	--	--	--	--	--	--	--	--	--	29
Macomb	1,768	--	--	--	440	41	--	--	--	--	--	1,287
Monroe	98	--	--	--	--	25	--	--	--	--	2	41
Montcalm	8,001	--	--	--	45	--	--	--	--	--	75	3,311
Muskegon	14,626	--	--	--	8	--	--	--	--	--	110	2,413
Oakland	624	--	--	--	--	--	--	--	--	--	29	205
Ottawa	4,346	--	--	--	626	--	--	--	--	--	26	790
Saginaw	532	--	--	--	70	--	--	--	--	--	30	49
Sanilac	1,905	--	--	--	223	10	--	--	--	--	--	1,341
St. Joseph	1,203	--	--	--	--	--	--	--	--	--	--	136
Tuscola	1,583	--	--	--	--	--	--	--	--	--	--	1,280
Van Buren	5,068	--	--	--	--	--	--	--	--	--	--	572
Washtenaw	252	8	60	8	90	0	1	14	--	--	1	--
Total	78,268	9	85	8	3,471	176	146	22	6	--	453	18,617
State total	2,658,049	4,245	79,314	63,141	198,788	50,907	8,587	74,144	19,242	5,498	35,808	846,379

(Table 5 continued on next page)

(Table 5 continued)

Forest Survey Unit and county[1]	Balsam poplar	Basswood	Beech	White birch	Yellow birch	Elm	Hickory	Hard maple	Soft maple	Red oak	White oak	Other hardwoods
Eastern Upper Peninsula												
Alger	1,194	1,247	2,886	3,880	1,859	69	--	15,285	14,144	576	--	1,062
Chippewa	1,745	978	1,803	2,993	1,316	73	--	10,391	10,964	499	--	673
Delta	1,666	943	2,764	3,322	1,637	11	--	13,530	12,047	412	--	985
Luce	1,961	1,690	2,788	5,349	2,094	241	--	18,896	18,114	1,888	440	1,110
Mackinac	1,736	891	1,770	3,447	1,188	27	--	9,354	12,908	478	--	643
Menominee	2,198	2,347	2,229	3,987	1,536	153	--	12,336	11,774	420	--	808
Schoolcraft	818	2,253	3,727	6,692	2,792	244	--	23,522	23,527	2,697	658	1,408
Total	11,317	10,350	17,966	29,670	12,421	818	--	103,315	103,478	6,971	1,098	6,688
Western Upper Peninsula												
Baraga	2,183	2,323	4,438	8,646	3,224	409	1	31,341	25,829	875	--	1,750
Dickinson	3,855	5,670	1,983	4,689	1,602	186	--	13,156	13,096	602	--	771
Gogebic	1,987	4,210	2,474	8,297	3,373	996	104	42,181	29,108	1,322	--	2,088
Houghton	2,096	3,166	2,107	5,313	2,610	167	5	20,302	14,340	1,524	1	841
Iron	3,682	3,126	2,079	7,385	2,007	482	1	16,234	16,897	666	--	811
Keweenaw	392	1,323	2,014	2,073	1,596	--	--	11,480	12,487	869	--	807
Marquette	6,334	2,106	6,551	9,049	3,822	160	--	34,299	28,794	768	--	2,380
Ontonagon	1,740	6,869	2,108	7,141	4,945	322	14	45,478	18,968	3,759	--	1,138
Total	22,268	28,793	23,755	52,593	23,180	2,722	125	214,471	159,519	10,386	1	10,585
Northern Lower Peninsula												
Alcona	897	216	155	1,755	1	0	--	797	4,039	6	--	192
Alpena	879	482	452	2,317	1	1	--	1,685	4,308	1,429	31	207
Antrim	616	1,477	352	1,233	132	133	223	3,552	6,553	7	13	804
Arenac	83	202	292	351	1	0	--	1,034	3,474	730	118	155
Bay	34	23	31	271	1	1	0	131	1,164	75	--	13
Benzie	115	717	639	45	21	23	42	3,266	6,050	48	76	801
Charlevoix	699	2,229	747	744	116	135	211	5,002	6,047	--	--	53
Cheboygan	673	3,022	660	2,463	57	14	7	3,488	6,241	52	--	282
Clare	405	311	347	525	74	80	147	2,008	6,082	1,383	234	187
Crawford	182	788	238	1,482	55	49	64	2,894	8,822	2,455	286	20
Emmet	38	2,721	631	1,401	28	20	10	3,588	4,851	9	2	258
Gladwin	123	107	132	381	22	24	44	662	5,104	973	992	74
Grand Traverse	175	239	192	78	32	34	64	954	2,262	112	206	922
Iosco	483	82	95	826	1	1	2	445	1,542	209	--	46
Isabella	256	129	49	190	47	50	93	634	2,565	144	159	--
Kalkaska	829	685	330	672	155	164	300	3,175	7,725	116	22	453
Lake	153	159	236	61	28	30	56	1,045	3,211	5,654	2,496	143
Leelanau	4	35	89	2	1	1	1	415	752	--	--	61
Manistee	19	190	483	78	4	4	7	1,747	4,750	1,128	224	356
Mason	379	317	409	149	69	75	137	2,108	5,059	418	104	231
Mecosta	414	224	116	189	76	82	150	1,156	3,265	242	284	25
Midland	446	431	462	1,009	91	94	161	2,438	9,255	129	193	230
Missaukee	888	798	341	673	162	174	321	3,344	9,296	209	71	90

County												
Montmorency	444	1,632	485	1,380	10	6	--	2,535	3,949	393	9	28
Newaygo	356	250	251	140	65	70	129	1,461	4,742	4,859	3,224	126
Oceana	531	293	170	209	97	105	192	1,528	3,933	411	359	46
Ogemaw	482	219	136	442	1	1	0	562	2,433	1,430	270	195
Osceola	490	333	320	362	89	96	178	2,070	5,773	830	1,037	156
Oscoda	178	287	61	788	0	0	--	1,182	2,697	221	34	--
Otsego	647	3,861	1,533	3,325	89	119	128	9,002	13,282	528	31	1,601
Presque Isle	736	627	363	2,846	20	13	--	1,364	5,143	114	3	24
Roscommon	189	126	95	1,032	24	25	45	642	7,169	4,323	1,665	27
Wexford	334	399	171	219	62	67	121	1,721	4,328	160	125	213
Total	13,177	23,613	11,065	27,639	1,631	1,693	2,833	67,635	165,866	28,795	12,265	8,017
Southern Lower Peninsula												
Allegan	56	28	11	22	10	11	20	137	3,502	2,757	3,059	--
Barry	87	44	17	34	16	17	31	215	520	12	24	--
Calhoun	--	--	--	--	--	--	--	--	690	582	629	--
Clinton	--	--	--	--	--	--	--	--	--	--	--	--
Gratiot	38	19	7	15	7	7	14	94	300	4	9	--
Huron	--	--	--	37	--	--	--	--	--	--	--	--
Ionia	14	7	--	6	3	3	5	36	87	38	77	--
Kalamazoo	1	1	3	0	--	--	0	3	2,542	2,150	2,334	--
Kent	205	107	49	80	37	40	74	537	3,285	1,706	2,114	7
Lapeer	--	--	--	--	--	--	--	--	--	--	--	--
Macomb	--	--	--	--	--	--	--	--	--	--	--	--
Monroe	5	3	1	2	1	1	2	12	29	--	--	--
Montcalm	173	88	36	78	32	34	63	443	1,892	1,072	632	1
Muskegon	191	107	64	76	35	38	70	900	3,218	3,546	3,833	18
Oakland	--	10	27	--	--	--	--	83	218	29	6	18
Ottawa	46	26	15	18	9	9	17	138	1,126	704	792	4
Saginaw	3	11	26	2	0	0	1	89	232	--	--	18
Sanilac	--	--	--	--	--	--	--	331	--	--	--	--
St. Joseph	--	--	--	--	--	--	--	387	387	327	353	--
Tuscola	--	--	--	--	--	--	--	303	--	--	--	--
Van Buren	--	--	--	--	--	--	--	1,632	1,632	1,377	1,488	--
Washtenaw	--	3	2	19	0	--	--	10	43	--	--	--
Total	818	454	255	389	149	161	297	2,696	20,337	14,303	15,348	66
State total	47,581	63,210	53,041	110,291	37,382	5,394	3,255	388,117	449,199	60,455	28,713	25,357

0 = Less than 1/2 cord.
[1] Includes only those counties that supplied pulpwood in 2004.
Table may not add due to rounding.

Table 6. -- Pulpwood production from roundwood by Forest Survey Unit, county, and species group, Minnesota, 2004

(In standard cords, unpeeled)

Forest Survey Unit and county [1]	All species	Species group									
		Northern white-cedar	Balsam fir	Jack pine	Red pine	White pine	Spruce	Tama-rack	Other softwoods	Ash	Aspen
Aspen-Birch											
Carlton	69,535	--	5,902	2,573	1,909	117	1,740	809	--	889	33,149
Cook	31,573	--	1,307	329	387	133	4,988	943	--	49	22,344
Koochiching	373,320	--	24,599	19,355	667	107	44,717	11,057	--	715	208,359
Lake	98,576	214	7,423	4,076	3,858	206	8,759	582	--	1,068	40,520
St. Louis	742,611	--	77,738	31,017	8,631	820	63,346	8,881	--	4,633	418,161
Total	1,315,615	214	116,968	57,350	15,452	1,383	123,550	22,271	--	7,353	722,533
Northern Pine											
Aitkin	142,394	--	6,742	4,603	3,293	290	4,142	2,215	--	1,775	92,408
Becker	49,335	--	324	2,085	601	1	251	568	--	17	41,149
Beltrami	198,338	--	5,080	25,167	976	16	2,746	2,184	--	1,569	136,551
Cass	137,272	--	3,099	8,563	4,111	43	1,316	1,462	--	824	95,384
Clearwater	77,897	--	1,183	3,481	178	1	311	200	--	122	63,621
Crow Wing	95,758	--	659	7,393	2,295	189	299	566	--	1,173	64,946
Hubbard	110,666	--	400	16,512	2,980	3	499	382	--	307	80,099
Itasca	323,081	--	27,352	10,252	8,618	122	22,163	3,895	74	2,534	197,311
Lake of the Woods	84,998	--	2,249	8,736	314	2	5,692	4,459	--	108	48,558
Mahnomen	17,257	--	30	1,132	--	--	62	54	--	--	14,221
Roseau	44,868	--	574	2,166	754	--	2,100	651	--	200	30,161
Wadena	12,917	--	6	2,327	671	--	--	--	--	--	9,674
Total	1,294,781	--	47,698	92,419	24,792	668	39,580	16,636	74	8,628	874,083
Central Hardwood											
Anoka	935	--	--	--	--	--	13	--	--	--	242
Benton	1,792	--	--	7	3	0	--	0	--	2	1,730
Chisago	433	--	15	7	24	0	--	1	--	2	187
Dakota	68	--	--	--	--	--	56	--	--	--	12
Douglas	1,580	--	211	11	--	--	38	--	--	--	1,170
Fillmore	12	--	12	--	--	--	--	--	--	--	--
Goodhue	120	--	10	--	--	--	--	--	--	5	12
Houston	224	--	--	--	--	--	--	--	--	10	--
Isanti	1,773	--	10	98	231	--	--	--	6	--	1,006
Kanabec	14,625	--	9	728	374	33	--	81	--	230	9,951
Mille Lacs	21,892	--	154	400	179	83	144	49	--	132	17,581
Morrison	19,092	--	94	488	282	48	30	31	--	105	15,581
Olmsted	13	--	--	--	--	--	3	--	--	--	9
Otter Tail	11,783	--	--	663	33	--	--	--	--	--	10,648
Pine	125,411	--	1,345	2,941	3,020	184	722	295	--	919	82,864
Sherburne	864	--	11	43	343	0	68	1	--	4	320
Stearns	59	1	--	4	2	--	--	0	--	1	32

Todd	2,897	--	--	101	--	--	--	--	--	--	2,781
Wabasha	1,124	--	--	21	1,103	--	--	--	--	--	--
Washington	3,172	--	482	9	4	0	150	1	--	3	1,806
Winona	776	--	--	--	584	0	--	147	--	--	--
Wright	227	--	--	15	7	--	--	1	--	5	134
Total	208,871	--	2,355	5,536	6,189	351	1,224	608	6	1,419	146,069
Prairie											
Clay	217	--	--	--	--	--	--	--	--	--	154
Kittson	17,979	--	--	449	--	--	101	106	--	--	15,870
Marshall	23,021	--	--	131	--	--	84	38	--	--	21,462
Norman	2,049	--	10	--	--	--	--	--	--	--	1,816
Pennington	7,584	--	5	--	--	--	7	--	--	33	7,291
Polk	4,180	--	--	--	--	--	--	--	--	--	4,035
Red Lake	1,297	--	27	--	14	--	--	--	--	--	1,098
Total	56,326	--	42	580	14	--	193	144	--	33	51,726
State total	2,875,593	214	167,063	155,884	46,446	2,402	164,547	39,659	80	17,433	1,794,411

(Table 6 continued on next page)

(Table 6 continued)

Forest Survey Unit and county [1]	Species group									
	Balsam poplar	Bass-wood	White birch	Cotton-wood [2]	Elm	Hard maple	Soft maple	Red oak	White oak	Other hardwoods
Aspen-Birch										
Carlton	525	998	13,530	--	133	2,404	4,701	--	--	158
Cook	26	48	697	--	7	71	236	--	--	8
Koochiching	37,903	724	22,945	--	5	1,845	317	--	--	6
Lake	1,042	3,193	20,113	--	85	1,665	5,672	--	--	101
St. Louis	26,816	3,345	65,810	--	396	11,542	20,878	91	36	471
Total	66,312	8,309	123,095	--	626	17,526	31,803	91	36	744
Northern Pine										
Aitkin	2,257	2,530	10,587	--	224	2,582	8,339	67	73	266
Becker	909	289	2,764	--	1	46	327	--	--	1
Beltrami	10,242	2,706	9,914	--	18	228	918	--	--	21
Cass	3,139	1,337	13,948	--	49	544	3,394	--	--	59
Clearwater	1,317	1,461	5,819	--	2	50	151	--	--	2
Crow Wing	697	1,524	7,306	--	180	1,844	6,456	8	8	214
Hubbard	890	366	7,368	--	4	62	790	--	--	5
Itasca	14,733	2,053	27,875	--	72	1,600	4,344	--	--	86
Lake of the Woods	8,890	18	5,399	--	3	476	90	--	--	3
Mahnomen	428	581	728	--	--	22	--	--	--	--
Roseau	5,710	--	2,371	--	--	180	--	--	--	--
Wadena	117	--	111	--	--	--	11	--	--	--
Total	49,329	12,865	94,189	--	553	7,634	24,820	75	80	657
Central Hardwood										
Anoka	--	167	217	--	--	92	204	--	--	--
Benton	21	3	9	--	0	4	12	--	--	0
Chisago	1	28	114	--	0	38	13	--	--	0
Dakota	--	--	--	--	--	--	--	--	--	--
Douglas	22	13	114	--	--	--	--	--	--	--
Fillmore	--	--	5	--	--	--	--	--	--	--
Goodhue	--	--	10	--	--	29	24	24	10	--
Houston	--	--	10	--	--	68	56	56	23	--
Isanti	--	197	32	--	--	50	104	18	19	--
Kanabec	144	264	1,003	--	38	388	1,338	--	--	45
Mille Lacs	103	785	786	--	21	334	1,018	47	51	25
Morrison	93	389	854	--	17	238	746	24	51	21
Olmsted	--	--	--	--	--	--	--	--	--	--
Otter Tail	397	--	42	--	--	--	--	--	--	--
Pine	559	1,397	18,710	--	147	5,178	6,767	120	68	175
Sherburne	6	5	31	--	1	7	23	--	--	1
Stearns	1	2	6	--	0	2	8	--	--	0

County									
Todd	14	--	--	--	--	--	--	--	--
Wabasha	--	--	--	--	--	--	--	--	--
Washington	2	170	228	0	97	220	--	--	0
Winona	--	--	33	--	11	--	--	--	--
Wright	3	5	20	1	8	27	--	--	1
Total	1,366	3,424	22,215	226	6,544	10,560	288	222	269
Prairie									
Clay	45	7	--	11	45	--	--	--	--
Kittson	929	--	478	--	12	--	--	--	--
Marshall	1,100	4	190	--	--	--	--	--	--
Norman	--	13	--	220	--	--	--	--	--
Pennington	76	--	1	166	--	--	--	--	--
Polk	47	--	11	82	--	--	--	--	--
Red Lake	20	34	6	98	--	--	--	--	--
Total	2,218	57	686	577	56	--	--	--	--
State total	119,225	24,655	240,185	1,405	31,762	67,183	453	339	1,670

0 = Less than 1/2 cord.

[1] Includes only those counties that supplied pulpwood in 2004.

Table may not add due to rounding.

Table 7.--Pulpwood production from roundwood by Forest Survey Unit, county, and species group, Wisconsin, 2004

(In standard cords, unpeeled)

Forest Survey Unit and county [1]	All species	Species group										
		Northern white-cedar	Balsam fir	Hemlock	Jack pine	Red pine	White pine	Spruce	Tamarack	Other softwoods	Ash	Aspen
Northeastern												
Florence	94,248	23	2,254	3,432	3,472	3,671	439	1,055	196	--	1,935	22,645
Forest	138,745	9	5,316	1,740	141	7,163	85	3,420	363	--	4,803	26,474
Langlade	184,191	--	7,142	324	78	1,722	237	4,939	1,058	--	7,267	41,947
Lincoln	176,886	--	4,769	588	1,527	2,884	757	2,647	803	--	6,115	66,617
Marinette	141,236	13	2,818	4,596	10,602	8,844	816	2,777	743	--	3,341	40,789
Menominee	57,854	1	188	11,304	161	2,345	1,731	37	1	--	2,211	9,297
Oconto	57,071	--	349	122	1,514	2,245	372	647	15	--	945	24,562
Oneida	175,538	--	6,209	286	8,023	7,138	1,795	8,312	1,814	--	4,200	67,277
Shawano	52,924	--	316	560	219	3,459	249	71	97	--	2,471	11,769
Vilas	88,067	--	2,840	172	6,026	4,954	1,709	1,884	489	--	2,280	31,206
Total	1,166,762	46	32,199	23,123	31,763	44,426	8,190	25,789	5,581	--	35,568	342,581
Northwestern												
Ashland	192,118	--	4,851	154	2,398	2,281	932	3,749	1,919	--	4,993	67,031
Barron	22,103	--	73	22	932	1,428	330	41	78	--	654	10,049
Bayfield	135,725	--	5,883	--	4,126	6,299	926	3,074	30	--	3,446	46,323
Burnett	53,190	--	113	63	7,861	2,211	9	--	3	--	686	23,192
Douglas	142,909	--	10,696	--	11,136	7,091	415	1,312	1,935	--	2,502	49,433
Iron	83,023	--	2,301	193	303	385	743	1,565	419	--	3,289	17,774
Polk	20,192	--	108	--	857	676	90	61	--	--	343	11,684
Price	154,127	--	8,394	1,732	779	1,098	356	6,499	3,359	--	4,972	53,468
Rusk	68,965	--	1,071	29	444	2,049	213	3,177	248	--	2,382	20,016
Sawyer	228,355	--	6,389	26	2,101	2,238	1,775	3,940	132	--	9,185	64,815
Taylor	94,264	--	1,991	729	3	684	51	1,816	278	--	3,532	35,037
Washburn	113,672	--	2,007	--	17,722	7,754	1,157	356	305	49	2,837	40,696
Total	1,308,644	--	43,877	2,885	48,662	34,194	6,997	25,590	8,706	49	38,821	439,518
Central												
Adams	68,385	--	--	--	19,015	23,792	6,476	55	144	--	584	4,179
Chippewa	33,151	--	84	--	150	1,918	374	518	84	--	1,033	14,882
Clark	72,039	--	53	63	3,341	2,367	996	146	--	--	1,577	41,138
Eau Claire	25,249	--	--	--	3,768	2,913	736	23	--	--	648	6,205
Jackson	64,894	--	9	--	11,878	8,402	3,273	48	16	--	1,409	11,941
Juneau	57,170	--	--	--	16,142	12,907	3,104	--	--	--	891	6,500
Marathon	92,105	--	977	2,967	1,034	6,856	880	1,024	16	--	3,255	35,874
Marquette	14,039	--	--	--	1,216	8,776	1,911	201	59	--	92	242
Monroe	22,243	--	--	15	6,103	3,366	1,672	57	99	--	413	2,649
Portage	50,129	--	310	326	7,567	12,190	4,019	152	561	--	926	9,393
Waupaca	127,871	--	41	39	181	7,243	1,521	373	23	--	1,437	18,124
Waushara	36,725	--	--	--	1,734	20,100	4,092	328	--	--	376	1,105
Wood	64,796	--	29	31	5,937	9,330	4,649	364	16	--	1,132	24,554
Total	728,796	--	1,504	3,440	78,068	120,158	33,702	3,289	1,017	--	13,773	176,786

Southwestern

Buffalo	3,316	—	—	126	501	171	126	—	70	576
Crawford	1,369	—	—	—	217	240	10	—	42	107
Dunn	16,008	32	—	1,248	2,587	498	309	—	335	3,592
Grant	1,546	—	—	25	915	132	159	—	7	217
Iowa	3,675	—	—	63	1,255	914	102	—	46	445
La Crosse	3,649	—	—	255	1,238	300	226	—	40	992
Lafayette	128	—	—	—	46	55	—	—	2	—
Pepin	719	3	—	115	328	24	38	—	1	181
Pierce	793	—	—	23	225	130	20	—	6	321
Richland	2,609	—	—	50	417	254	—	—	109	351
Sauk	7,350	40	—	525	3,207	592	630	—	85	672
St. Croix	4,907	—	—	526	1,750	54	186	—	46	1,577
Trempealeau	6,994	—	—	228	2,736	863	293	—	88	624
Vernon	1,349	—	—	30	650	324	—	—	5	248
Total	54,413	75	—	3,215	16,072	4,552	2,099	—	881	9,902

Southeastern

Brown	1,126	—	—	32	638	26	—	—	26	108
Calumet	219	53	—	—	—	—	—	13	10	28
Columbia	6,715	—	—	184	3,661	572	35	—	91	472
Dane	611	—	—	16	180	157	47	—	5	34
Dodge	2,191	—	—	—	26	—	10	—	31	76
Door	5,078	39	122	14	51	302	123	—	163	2,353
Fond Du Lac	4,332	—	—	51	1,079	1,103	61	—	17	76
Green	281	—	—	12	168	24	—	—	3	14
Green Lake	7,250	—	—	19	1,056	664	83	—	74	2,948
Jefferson	535	—	—	—	170	53	199	—	2	—
Kewaunee	1,333	—	—	10	549	83	34	—	40	196
Manitowoc	2,446	17	—	—	133	505	—	1,079	39	28
Milwaukee	10	—	—	—	—	—	—	—	1	—
Outagamie	3,676	—	—	—	345	111	—	—	179	722
Ozaukee	61	—	—	—	14	13	11	—	2	—
Rock	648	—	—	—	391	157	—	—	5	—
Sheboygan	934	—	—	—	265	58	452	—	10	25
Walworth	184	—	—	—	19	11	28	—	8	27
Washington	962	—	—	16	186	27	66	—	35	68
Waukesha	1,443	—	—	—	955	345	24	—	8	—
Winnebago	3,487	—	18	21	208	643	31	—	41	198
Total	43,526	109	139	374	10,092	4,855	1,207	1,092	791	7,373
State total	3,302,141	46	77,764	29,586	162,082	58,297	57,974	49	89,835	976,161

(Table 7 continued on next page)

(Table 7 continued)

Forest Survey Unit and county [1]	Species group												
	Balsam poplar	Bass-wood	Beech	White birch	Yellow birch	Cotton-wood	Elm	Hickory	Hard maple	Soft maple	Red oak	White oak	Other hardwoods
Northeastern													
Florence	692	3,408	2,530	5,585	2,548	--	260	29	18,112	18,961	1,821	79	1,100
Forest	276	9,161	2,497	14,218	3,293	--	1,234	9	26,142	27,653	3,428	310	1,009
Langlade	38	12,431	2,585	17,966	4,032	--	1,615	50	36,963	35,611	5,888	1,068	1,230
Lincoln	3	4,578	549	14,872	4,545	--	545	447	35,679	25,210	1,619	338	1,796
Marinette	1,733	7,439	1,659	9,108	2,403	--	760	--	19,839	18,927	3,058	284	688
Menominee	5	2,483	315	3,449	1,339	--	210	47	11,296	7,363	3,568	328	175
Oconto	1,008	1,860	1,106	2,658	1,047	--	163	1	8,249	8,657	1,020	85	447
Oneida	32	2,967	897	17,098	3,307	--	919	215	21,532	19,520	2,578	324	1,096
Shawano	4	1,121	160	3,089	557	--	212	17	12,936	9,007	4,968	1,574	69
Vilas	54	1,368	133	10,187	1,397	--	462	99	10,282	8,977	2,797	330	424
Total	3,843	46,817	12,430	98,229	24,467	--	6,380	914	201,030	179,885	30,744	4,721	8,034
Northwestern													
Ashland	1,757	5,918	27	15,879	978	--	1,930	7	37,269	34,246	3,560	948	1,291
Barron	7	282	1	1,204	88	--	92	--	1,911	2,899	1,551	450	11
Bayfield	472	3,627	5	17,980	594	--	1,031	11	17,534	19,080	3,694	921	667
Burnett	95	563	--	6,826	51	--	156	--	3,521	4,097	2,914	766	127
Douglas	409	2,941	9	18,547	369	--	677	19	15,195	17,002	1,996	616	609
Iron	150	2,636	195	11,743	1,570	--	1,012	58	19,842	15,355	2,470	506	514
Polk	4	464	--	1,527	103	--	105	--	1,296	1,684	982	203	6
Price	33	7,250	150	18,971	2,294	--	1,420	90	21,165	18,305	2,912	450	429
Rusk	33	1,588	26	8,765	608	--	445	22	10,574	10,307	5,136	1,710	122
Sawyer	302	6,811	79	26,830	1,661	--	1,870	5	39,215	37,692	17,309	5,535	446
Taylor	--	3,470	118	12,926	1,092	--	813	32	16,947	11,703	2,421	493	127
Washburn	222	3,502	2	10,637	272	10	389	--	8,696	10,054	5,090	1,770	145
Total	3,484	39,052	614	151,835	9,679	10	9,941	245	193,165	182,426	50,034	14,367	4,493
Central													
Adams	--	49	2	781	35	--	29	--	3,224	2,761	5,453	1,806	--
Chippewa	0	781	10	3,318	272	--	253	2	3,322	3,618	2,092	430	9
Clark	1	915	52	3,086	339	--	290	1	6,757	5,678	4,024	1,192	24
Eau Claire	--	277	6	1,725	191	--	167	2	2,415	2,350	3,193	621	9
Jackson	--	328	2	3,038	189	--	163	3	7,035	6,303	8,450	2,397	11
Juneau	--	116	1	1,028	31	--	19	1	5,201	4,376	4,905	1,943	5
Marathon	--	2,084	219	4,513	724	--	435	23	15,491	10,949	3,376	1,246	162
Marquette	--	7	3	119	18	--	5	--	489	402	356	140	2
Monroe	--	44	--	547	22	--	20	--	2,304	1,973	2,197	763	1
Portage	--	386	12	2,068	218	--	181	2	3,856	3,694	3,200	1,046	23
Waupaca	--	4,986	83,987	1,353	171	--	134	--	3,960	2,775	1,229	289	6
Waushara	--	13	3	432	44	--	4	4	2,259	1,857	3,555	802	16
Wood	1	499	6	2,262	190	--	176	2	5,245	4,749	4,115	1,500	7
Total	2	10,485	84,303	24,271	2,443	--	1,876	41	61,559	51,486	46,144	14,173	276

Southwestern

County	1	2	3	4	5	6	7	8	9	10	11	12	13
Buffalo	--	21	--	465	14	13	--	--	305	290	530	109	--
Crawford	--	5	--	61	3	3	--	--	229	200	180	71	--
Dunn	0	322	6	980	180	87	11	--	1,414	1,430	2,470	463	43
Grant	--	4	--	23	2	2	--	--	23	25	9	2	--
Iowa	--	3	--	56	2	2	--	--	265	224	214	84	--
La Crosse	--	14	--	93	9	8	--	--	171	159	108	36	--
Lafayette	--	1	--	4	--	--	--	--	11	7	1	--	--
Pepin	--	1	--	3	--	--	--	--	3	9	11	1	--
Pierce	--	4	--	19	2	2	--	--	17	21	4	--	--
Richland	--	53	--	323	33	32	--	--	359	394	175	57	--
Sauk	--	11	0	131	8	7	--	--	445	389	468	138	--
St. Croix	2	31	--	206	14	16	--	--	166	273	48	11	2
Trempealeau	--	39	--	558	27	23	1	--	319	328	698	168	2
Vernon	--	--	--	5	--	--	--	--	29	24	23	10	--
Total	2	509	7	2,927	295	196	13	--	3,756	3,773	4,941	1,151	47

Southeastern

County	1	2	3	4	5	6	7	8	9	10	11	12	13
Brown	4	14	0	76	10	8	--	--	84	83	15	2	2
Calumet	--	--	2	11	9	--	--	--	59	34	--	--	--
Columbia	--	23	1	197	30	14	2	--	445	394	464	124	7
Dane	--	--	--	5	--	--	--	--	36	30	81	19	--
Dodge	63	61	--	100	20	9	2	--	117	114	1,458	163	4
Door	--	86	6	506	72	52	--	--	499	525	93	10	--
Fond Du Lac	--	47	0	26	12	--	2	--	111	83	1,484	176	4
Green	--	1	--	6	--	--	--	--	19	16	14	5	--
Green Lake	--	49	--	59	48	7	2	--	230	365	1,457	166	23
Jefferson	--	--	--	6	4	--	--	--	26	18	49	7	1
Kewaunee	1	8	6	72	25	5	--	--	171	121	9	1	--
Manitowoc	--	2	2	49	6	1	--	--	213	173	143	55	--
Milwaukee	--	--	0	1	1	--	--	--	5	3	--	--	--
Outagamie	--	56	15	334	103	23	7	--	947	648	140	19	27
Ozaukee	--	--	0	2	1	--	--	--	11	6	--	--	--
Rock	--	--	--	5	--	--	--	--	29	25	25	10	--
Sheboygan	--	3	0	22	3	2	--	--	36	35	18	5	--
Walworth	--	--	2	8	6	--	--	--	43	24	8	--	--
Washington	--	2	4	71	39	1	4	--	233	158	36	3	14
Waukesha	--	1	1	13	6	--	--	--	48	30	10	--	1
Winnebago	--	53	--	76	15	4	2	--	218	185	1,565	206	4
Total	68	407	41	1,646	409	127	22	10	3,579	3,068	7,068	972	85
State total	7,400	97,271	97,394	278,908	37,293	18,519	1,233	10	463,090	420,637	138,931	35,385	12,936

0 = Less than 1/2 cord.
1 Includes only those counties that supplied pulpwood in 2004.
Table may not add due to rounding.

Table 8.--Number of industrial pulp or particleboard plants in the Lake States by product form, species group used, and State, 2004

Product form and species group	Total Lake States	State		
		Michigan	Minnesota	Wisconsin
Roundwood				
Softwoods				
Northern white-cedar	3	2	1	0
Balsam fir	18	4	8	6
Hemlock	4	1	0	3
Jack pine	15	4	6	5
Red pine	16	4	6	6
White pine	14	4	5	5
Spruce	17	2	9	6
Tamarack	10	1	5	4
Other softwoods	3	1	2	0
Total plants using softwoods [1]	25	4	13	8
Hardwoods				
Ash	23	7	5	11
Aspen	35	11	13	11
Balsam poplar	15	6	8	1
Basswood	22	9	9	4
Beech	11	7	0	4
White birch	29	8	10	11
Yellow birch	11	6	0	5
Cottonwood	1	0	1	0
Elm	6	2	1	3
Hickory	2	1	0	1
Hard maple	24	9	4	11
Soft maple	28	10	7	11
Red oak	15	8	1	6
White oak	10	4	1	5
Other hardwoods	9	5	1	3
Total plants using hardwoods [1]	42	12	13	17
Total plants using roundwood [1]	43	12	14	17
Residues				
Softwood	11	2	3	6
Hardwood	20	7	5	8
Total plants using residues [1]	21	7	5	9
Total plants [1]	44	12	14	18

[1] Some plants use more than one species, so numbers in columns are not additive.

Table 9.--Average daily production of active wood pulp mills in the Lake States by State, company, location, and type of pulp produced, 2004

(In tons per 24 hours)

State and company	Location	Average daily production	Type of pulp produced					
			Sulfite	Kraft	Kraft/ groundwood	Groundwood/ mechanical	Semi-chemical	Thermo-mechanical
Michigan								
Decorative Panels International, Inc.	Alpena	250	--	--	--	250	--	--
International Paper Co.	Quinnesec	1,250	--	1,250	--	--	--	--
Meadwestvaco Corp.	Escanaba	1,273	--	--	1,273	--	--	--
Menasha Packaging Co. LLC	Otsego	660	--	--	--	--	660	--
Packaging Corp. Of America	Filer City	361	--	--	--	--	361	--
Sappi Fine Paper	Muskegon	344	--	344	--	--	--	--
Smurfit-Stone Container Corp.	Ontonagon	751	--	--	--	--	751	--
Total	7 mills	4,889	--	1,594	1,273	250	1,772	--
Minnesota								
Boise White Paper, LLC.	International Falls	1,150	--	1,150	--	--	--	--
Certainteed Corp.	Shakopee	310	--	--	--	310	--	--
Georgia-Pacific Corp.	Duluth	210	--	--	--	--	--	210
International Bildrite, Inc.	International Falls	100	--	--	--	100	--	--
International Paper Co.	Sartell	423	--	--	--	--	--	423
Sapppi, LLC	Cloquet	1,269	--	1,269	--	--	--	--
Stora Enso North America	Proctor	325	--	--	--	325	--	--
UPM - Blandin	Grand Rapids	410	--	--	--	410	--	--
Total	8 mills	4,197	--	2,419	--	1,145	--	633
Wisconsin								
Domtar Industries, Inc.	Nekoosa	495	--	495	--	--	--	--
Domtar Industries, Inc.	Port Edwards	255	255	--	--	--	--	--
Fraser Papers	Park Falls	170	170	--	--	--	--	--
Georgia-Paicfic Corp.	Phillips	90	--	--	--	90	--	--
International Paper Co.	Kaukauna	450	--	450	--	--	--	--
Mule-Hide Manufacturing	Cornell	130	--	--	--	--	--	130
Packaging Corp. Of America	Tomahawk	1,378	--	--	--	--	1,378	--
Stora Enso North America	Biron	400	--	--	--	--	--	400
Stora Enso North America	Niagara	250	--	--	--	250	--	--
Stora Enso North America	Stevens Point	200	--	--	--	--	--	200
Stora Enso North America	Wisconsin Rapids	1,200	--	1,200	--	--	--	--
Wausau Mosinee Paper	Mosinee	250	--	250	--	--	--	--
Wausau Paper	Brokaw	222	222	--	--	--	--	--
Weyerhaeuser Co.	Rothschild	160	160	--	--	--	--	--
Total	14 mills	5,650	807	2,395	--	340	1,378	730
Lake States total	29 mills	14,736	807	6,408	1,273	1,735	3,150	1,363

Table 10.--Annual production of active particleboard and panel mills in the Lake States by State, company, location, and product produced, 2004

(In million square feet 3/4-inch basis)

State and company	Location	Product produced	Annual production
Michigan			
GFP Strandwood Corp.	Hancock	Molded oriented strand board	2
Georgia-Pacific Corp.	Gaylord	Particleboard	229
Louisiana-Pacific Corp.	Newberry	Oriented strand board	72
Louisiana-Pacific Corp.	Sagola	Oriented strand board	185
Weyerhaeuser Co.	Grayling	Oriented strand board	250
Total	5 mills		738
Minnesota			
Ainsworth Engineered (USA), LLC	Bemidji	Oriented strand board	265
Ainsworth Engineered (USA), LLC	Cook	Oriented strand board	207
Ainsworth Engineered (USA), LLC	Grand Rapids	Oriented strand board	167
Louisiana-Pacific Corp.	Two Harbors	Oriented strand board	67
Norbord Minnesota	Solway	Oriented strand board	218
Trus Joist - Weyerhaeuser	Deerwood	Engineered wood product	n/a
Total	6 mills		924
Wisconsin			
Louisiana-Pacific Corp.	Hayward	Oriented strand board	250
Louisiana-Pacific Corp.	Tomahawk	Oriented strand board	65
Marshfield Doorsystems	Marshfield	Particleboard	79
Rodman Industries	Marinette	Particleboard	8
Total	4 mills		402
Lake States total	15 mills		2,064

Table 11.–Production and imports of pulpwood, Central States, 2004

(In standard cords, unpeeled)

Product form, species group, and destination	Production by State[1]				Regional total	Imports		Total Imports	Total receipts
	Illinois	Indiana	Iowa	Missouri		Lake States	Other U.S.		
Roundwood									
Softwoods									
Lake States	1,072	--	--	--	1,072	--	--	--	--
Northeastern States	44	2,042	--	--	2,086	--	--	--	--
Southern States	696	--	--	--	696	--	--	--	--
Total	1,812	2,042	--	--	3,854	--	--	--	--
Soft hardwoods[2]									
Central States	1,976	6,586	1,690	4,859	15,112	--	--	--	15,112
Northeastern States	--	150	--	--	150	--	--	--	--
Southern States	5,669	2,117	--	7,316	15,102	--	--	--	--
Total	7,645	8,853	1,690	12,175	30,363	--	--	--	15,112
Hard hardwoods[3]									
Central States	2,877	9,588	3,187	587	16,240	--	--	--	16,240
Northeastern States	--	65	--	--	65	--	--	--	--
Southern States	10,247	6,701	--	98,681	115,629	--	--	--	--
Total	13,124	16,355	3,187	99,268	131,934	--	--	--	16,240
Total all roundwood									
Central States	4,853	16,174	4,878	5,447	31,351	--	--	--	31,351
Lake States	1,072	--	--	--	1,072	--	--	--	--
Northeastern States	44	2,258	--	--	2,301	--	--	--	--
Southern States	16,612	8,818	--	105,996	131,426	--	--	--	--
Total	22,581	27,250	4,878	111,443	166,151	--	--	--	31,351
Residues									
Softwoods									
Central States	--	--	--	--	--	--	26,800	26,800	26,800
Northeastern States	--	268	--	--	268	--	--	--	--
Southern States	--	--	--	803	803	--	--	--	--
Total	--	268	--	803	1,071	--	26,800	26,800	26,800
Hardwoods									
Central States	5,504	40,844	17,975	13,071	77,395	3,833	--	3,833	81,228
Lake States	--	10,594	1,778	--	12,372	--	--	--	--
Northeastern States	--	7,004	--	--	7,004	--	--	--	--
Southern States	10,313	72,990	--	136,693	219,996	--	--	--	--
Total	15,818	131,432	19,753	149,764	316,767	3,833	--	3,833	81,228
Total all residues									
Central States	5,504	40,844	17,975	13,071	77,395	3,833	26,800	30,633	108,028
Lake States	--	10,594	1,778	--	12,372	--	--	--	--
Northeastern States	--	7,272	--	--	7,272	--	--	--	--
Southern States	10,313	72,990	--	137,496	220,799	--	--	--	--
Total	15,818	131,699	19,753	150,568	317,838	3,833	26,800	30,633	108,028
Total all wood material									
Central States	10,358	57,018	22,853	18,518	108,746	3,833	26,800	30,633	139,379
Lake States	1,072	10,594	1,778	--	13,444	--	--	--	--
Northeastern States	44	9,530	--	--	9,573	--	--	--	--
Southern States	26,925	81,808	--	243,492	352,225	--	--	--	--
Total	38,398	158,949	24,631	262,010	483,989	3,833	26,800	30,633	139,379

[1]Vertical columns of figures under the box heading "Production by State" present the amount of roundwood cut or residue generated in each State.

[2]Hardwood species with an average specific gravity of 0.50 or less.

[3]Hardwood species with an average specific gravity greater than 0.50.

Table may not add due to rounding

Table 12.--Central States pulpwood production by product form
and species group, 2000-2004

(In standard cords, unpeeled)

Product form and species group	2000	2001	2002	2003	2004
Roundwood					
Softwoods	7,643	2,110	3,432	5,485	3,854
Soft hardwoods[1]	64,036	50,939	25,783	31,393	30,363
Hard hardwoods[2]	165,994	113,062	121,600	113,501	131,934
Total	237,673	166,111	150,815	150,380	166,151
Residues					
Softwood	12,849	117	1,860	1,860	1,071
Hardwood	269,603	302,510	274,219	310,161	316,767
Total	282,452	302,627	276,079	312,021	317,838
Total all wood material	520,125	468,738	426,895	462,400	483,989

[1] Hardwood species with an average specific gravity of 0.50 or less.
[2] Hardwood species with an average specific gravity greater than 0.50.

Table may not add due to rounding.

50

Table 13.--Central States pulpwood production by State and destination, 2000-2004

(In thousand standard cords, unpeeled)

Year	Illinois			Indiana			Iowa			Missouri		
		Destination			Destination			Destination			Destination	
	Total	Central States	Other States	Total	Central States	Other States	Total	Central States	Other States	Total	Central States	Other States
2000	92	32	60	168	70	98	48	46	1	212	17	195
2001	75	22	53	160	67	93	44	43	1	190	14	175
2002	59	9	50	135	54	82	30	29	1	202	14	188
2003	44	10	35	154	53	101	25	23	2	239	19	221
2004	38	10	28	159	57	102	25	23	2	262	19	243
5-year average	62	17	45	155	60	95	34	33	1	221	17	204

Table may not add due to rounding.

Table 14.--Average daily production of active wood pulp mills in the Central States by company, location, and type of pulp produced, 2004

(In tons per 24 hours)

Company	Location	Average daily production	Type of pulp produced		
			Groundwood/ mechanical	Semi- chemical	Thermo- mechanical
International Paper Co.	Terre Haute, Indiana	250	--	250	--
Box USA	Fort Madison, Iowa	158	--	158	--
Jeld-Wen Fiber Of Iowa	Dubuque, Iowa	76	76	--	--
Huebert Brothers Products, LLC	Booneville, Missouri	80	--	--	80
Central States total	4 mills	564	76	408	80